When Glamour Meets Gratitude

When Glamour Meets Gratitude

Your Style Companion to a Healthy Self Image

Jennifer Stepanik

Copyright © 2023 by Jennifer Stepanik.

ISBN: 978-0-6482251-3-3

All rights reserved. No part of this book may be reproduced or transmitted in any form or by any means, electronic or mechanical, including photocopying, recording, or by any information storage and retrieval system, without permission in writing from the copyright owner.

This book was printed in the United States of America.

Contents

Introduction 7

1. Feet, Ankles & Shoes 15
2. Legs, The Golden Ratio & Hosiery 30
3. A Brief Introduction to Body Types 39
4. Thighs, Hips and Buttocks; Skirts, Pants and Jeans 42
5. The Reproductive Organs and Underwear Styles 76
6. The Back, Power Posture and Backless Dressing 89
7. The Waistline, Your Belly and Dresses 100
8. Bust, Bras, the Breath and Necklines 120
9. Shoulders, Stress and Sleeves 141
10. Arms and Hands - and Wrist Enhancements 154
11. Neck and Throat; Scarves and Scarf Styles 167
12. Face, Skin and Foundation 176
13. Lips, Nose, Cheekbones 186
14. Eyes, Ears and Brows 202
15. Hair and Styling 220
16. Becoming Resourceful 235
17. On Fitting In and Measuring Up 250
18. Showing Up and Your Sense of Style 259
19. The final touches-Personal Creativity, Doing what you love,
    Self -Worth and Sharing yourself with others 324

Resources 335

Introduction

When *Glamour Meets Gratitude* has been written to help you recognise just how beautiful you already are.

After spending close to twenty years in the industry I call 'glamour', where glamour is defined as an *appearance of enhanced attractiveness*, I wanted to find a way of adding a sense of groundedness to an arena that might otherwise be considered superficial.

The ways I hope to achieve this purpose are by introducing four key concepts:

1. Gratitude
2. Resourcefulness
3. Measuring Up and Fitting In
4. Showing up

As you read through the book these concepts will start to make a lot more sense. I believe they are necessary, if you want to navigate through the barrage of marketing messages about what is considered fashionable, 'in' or socially acceptable.

These concepts will assist you to understand and acknowledge your own unique sense of style, and to excavate the beauty that was always present within you. I hope you will come to see that it was just a case of giving yourself the attention and appreciation you required, in order to see it.

This book is divided into two separate sections: Your Body and Your Style. In Your Body we will be giving each and every body part the recognition and celebration it deserves. Each part of you will be acknowledged and loved, and options will be provided about how that part of your body can be enhanced, including hair, makeup and styling advice.

This is followed by Your Style. This section covers the principles of styling according to your body type; it covers wardrobe essentials, how to maximise your current wardrobe, how to recognise your personal style, how to understand colour; it looks at proportion and measurements that matter, and also addresses how you show up in the world.

By the end of this book, I want to ensure that you walk away feeling a lot more secure in your understanding about how to apply the principles of glamour to your personal body shape and style, as well as how to truly appreciate the body, face and hair you were given.

The glamour industry has an important place in society. This domain provides us with a space to take care of ourselves, to embellish ourselves and to express ourselves creatively.

Having spent a considerable time in this industry, I've seen the lengths that some people go to in order to fit a 'socially acceptable mould of beauty'.

You can nip, tuck, alter and inject and completely manipulate what is already there. Now I'm not about to go on an anti-injectables rant; it serves a purpose. The issue I have is when I see women walk in the door looking one way and then walk in a few months later looking completely different. They begin to lose their essence after undergoing multiple procedures. They become so fixated on the physical angle that they forget the most essential ingredient to beauty—and that is your energy.

I've seen this situation happen with makeup application as well. All the highlighting, contouring and false lashes have become a mask for a certain number of women. It's true that it has a completely face-transforming effect … however this comes at the detriment of losing what was already there.

Makeup and injectables, done well, can help enhance your beauty. However, this doesn't happen when you're coming from a place of not enough; it happens when you come from a place of gratitude and acceptance of what you already have.

I've seen people spend hours trying to make themselves 'pretty', wear the most trendy and sophisticated designer label item of clothing in order to look a certain way, to fit in, or, more often, to look like someone else entirely.

The age-old saying, beauty comes from within' isn't there to confuse you. It's there because it's true, and it needs to be your starting place. Instead

Introduction

of focusing on what don't I like about myself or what feature somebody else has that I don't have, you need to look in the mirror and ask the question, 'What do I like most about myself? What areas do I want to enhance?'

> *Real beauty is the acknowledgement and appreciation of what is ... not a comparison to... or an excuse about... or any other 'not quite good enough yet' statement.*

It's very rare to find someone who totally 'gets it' when it comes to their unique sense of style. Often, the reason is because people spend so long looking outward, at what others are doing with their hair, makeup and clothing, that they never really bother to enquire who they are and what they are all about. The end result is always the same ... and it's not quite right.

The handful of women who do take the time to understand what they like—who they really are, what they are all about, what suits them and their personal sense of style—are the ones who really turn heads.

So what's the difference between the two? One looked inwards as their starting point and the other looked outwards—to the celebrity, to the popular girl—and this means they are starting from a point of comparison and often lack.

Until you can look in the mirror and see the beauty that has always been present, you will struggle to achieve what you really desire.

I started this book with the goal of fusing two aspects of being: feeling great about yourself on the inside—having a healthy self-esteem and self-worth—with looking amazing on the outside—glamour.

> *We are all perfect until we start to compare ourselves to others ... it's time to focus on your own perfection!*

And, yes, we each play a number of roles in our lives—from disco diva to social event hostess, from soccer mum to corporate executive. Each of these roles requires a different outfit to assist you to even play the role you've been assigned.

My concern, however, is when I see people fixate on the external—on the outfit and the makeup for their role—in order to feel there's any hope of them being acceptble or feeling good enough.

Clothes, hair and makeup definitely have a confidence-building effect when put together well. However, when you rely upon the externals for self-confidence and esteem you will only ever gain a temporary boost … and at a very hefty price tag! Your self-confidence and self-esteem will come from other people's compliments, rather than from the opinion that matters the most … your own.

Rather than relying on the externals of dress to make you feel good about yourself, I would like to propose a more holistic approach.

Yes, you need to wear clothes; yes, you need to gain an understanding of what works best for your shape, your colouring and your unique sense of style. However, if you were to focus your attention on building your self-esteem, your confidence and your feelings of self-worth as the foundation upon which to start creating your wardrobe, you may find that you encounter a love affair with your wardrobe and yourself that comes from within rather than without. This is a much healthier starting point, and it's the point at which I wish to start this book.

So, I ask you to hold back all judgement whilst reading this book, as it is a little different from your standard 'How-to-Look-Stylish Manual'. This is going to go a little deeper and will require a little self-reflection, appreciation and awareness, as well as a shift in the way you've been thinking about yourself and your wardrobe until now.

Perhaps, in the past, you found yourself plastering on makeup like it's a mask, and searching for the trendiest and highest-ticket clothing items to make you feel more socially valuable and worthwhile.

Yes, models and movie stars are a great source of inspiration for wardrobe ideas but making a style your own is much more important than trying to look like the so-called social ideal portrayed on the cover of yet another magazine.

In any case, the social ideal is simply *one version* of beautiful. There are so many alternative versions of beauty in the world just waiting to be explored, acknowledged and appreciated. Beauty isn't a fixed concept assigned only to people blessed with certain physical dimensions. Remember that the skinniness emphasised in most models today wasn't

Introduction

even considered beautiful until Twiggy came along in the 1960s. *Beauty is in all of us just waiting to be recognised and expressed.*

> *'My issue with what they consider beautiful, is their concept of beauty centres around excluding people'* — Rupi Kaur, Milk and Honey.

Imagine starting your day from a more authentic, happy, grateful, confident, loving and joyful place. This starting point would naturally make you feel and appear more radiant and beautiful.

So, how do you go about discovering your beauty, in order to express it more fully? Simple, you shift your focus and perspective. Rather than using the media and magazines as a starting point, you need to refocus and begin by making a really honest and healthy assessment of yourself. From the point of view of yourself … rather than in comparison to others.

I invite you to begin the practice of greater appreciation for who you are and the package you've been given.

The knowledge I have of the body and how it functions has been gained from many years working as a remedial massage therapist and reflexologist, as well as years of dedicated yoga practise.

Too often we criticize and whine about parts of ourselves that we don't consider perfect. It's important to realise that we are all incredibly beautiful, if we only take the time to see and acknowledge our true beauty.

> *Our essence of beauty is something that will never be discovered through comparison, but only through self-awareness and gratitude.*

PART 1
Your Body

Chapter 1

Feet, Ankles & Shoes

Let's begin with your feet

THE FEET

Start at your little pinky toe on your right foot, and then bring your awareness to all of your toes on both of your feet. Now move your gaze over the whole of your feet.

Pay attention, firstly, to the purpose that your feet and toes serve. Your feet and toes are responsible for helping you to stand firm, with perfect balance, each and every day. They also assist you in moving forward with certainty and ease. Your feet keep you grounded and solid … feel into this groundedness. Really explore the sensations of the feet. Are they hot or cold? Is there a tingling or a heavy sensation? Do they ache in certain areas? Are they tender or rough at the heels?

At this stage I want you to simply be grateful for their function and their form. Yes, that means you say, 'Thank you, feet and toes,' and not, 'I hate my feet' or 'my toes are ugly'). Just say thank you. Resist the urge to complain or criticise for the duration of this practice. Have you ever seen a baby turn their nose up at their feet? No, they're fascinated by their feet. They play with them; they smell them; they even eat them, if they can. I'm not advising you stick your feet in your mouth … but, you get my point. If you don't get it, my point is that at one point in your life you were so fascinated by yourself that you were willing to consume the very things you now reject … so what happened?

Criticism and comparison happened, and it filled the space of love and fascination that you had for yourself. It's time to return to that space.

Now, ask yourself what could you do for these toes to make them step forward with greater poise and grace? Is there a physical way you could demonstrate appreciation for them? Perhaps consider giving them a file or polish before selecting the perfect pair of shoes to step into before you start your day.

Is there dryness in the heel? Are you digging in and being too stubborn about a particular issue? Could you relax your stance and just trust that your future has a certainty about it, one that you must allow for in order to stand firmly in your own power, instead of feeling the need to ground down and fight?

Is a pedicure in order? Could you apply a heel balm or lotion to your feet, to demonstrate your gratitude for your feet and toes? *If you were suddenly visited by a genie and turned into a pair of feet ... how exactly would you like to be cared for?*

Consider taking your feet out for a stroll at the end of the day, perhaps you could take them into nature—to a park or to a beach. This could be your symbolic grounding gesture for your feet. Even walking barefoot in the back yard or garden will do.

If you're in an apartment surrounded by concrete, then a bowl of warm water with Epsom salts will suffice. Simply getting into the habit of appreciating your feet whilst connecting to nature will help ground you. The sense of calm and presence generated by focusing your attention on your feet isn't emphasised enough in our manic and overworked culture.

The act of focusing on your feet will assist you to slow down your mind; it will enable you to send your worries down into the earth or the water, purifying your mind and body of all of the toxic thoughts that may have been ravaging it throughout the day. Essentially, through practising these grounding exercises daily you will be:

- allowing yourself the space and time to centre and ground your thoughts, as well as become present in the moment.
- allowing the mind to send your negative thoughts and concerns into the earth. The earth is an amazing recycler of energy; it takes waste—think of the way compost is converted into new, fertile

soil—and creates new life. Trees grow through the nourishment of soil.
- enabling self-connection. The main goal of meditation and yoga techniques is just that … to create a stronger connection with your own self.

If you find yourself too much in your head or suffering from insomnia, if you feel unsettled, if fear and worry keep surfacing, then the practice of appreciating your feet will promote a sense of calm. Asking your feet and toes where they want to be, or where they want to go and how they wish to be treated and displayed will encourage the tranquility and quiet that are often neglected in this hectic world.

Start and end your day at your feet every day, instead of in your head. A foot soak—rather than a blue screen on your computer or mobile—before bed will have you sleeping like a baby. Step into your morning with gratitude for the service your feet and toes provide you daily. Your connectedness will also grow in many ways as you become more grounded.

CALMING FOOT SOAKS

To really pay homage to your feet here is a simple foot soak recipe:

- Warm water in a foot bowl
- 1 cup of Epsom Salts

You can customise the scent of your foot soak with any of the following essential oils, using a maximum ratio of 10 drops essential oil to 1 cup of salts:

- Lavender oil (calming, antibacterial and regenerative)
- Chamomile oil (for relaxation)
- Lemon oil (antibacterial with powerful cleansing properties)
- Peppermint oil (contains menthol, which has a refreshing effect on tired feet, as well as being antibacterial)

THE ANKLES

Now I would like you to move your awareness up a little, to your ankles. Look at their form. When you really pay attention to what sits below the surface of the skin here you'll see that this is a very delicate area of a few bones—your heel bones—bound to your leg bones by ligaments that allow for an incredible range of motion.

The hind foot joint enables your ankle to move from side to side. It also allows you to twist your foot inwards (inversion) and outwards (eversion).

Your ankle bones are then attached to your leg bones at the ankle joint, which acts like a hinge and facilitates the up and down movement of the foot, with the assistance of the leg muscles. It is almost as though the muscles of the legs act as puppeteers of the ankle joint. Essentially, your ankles serve the purposes of enabling us to walk, run and jump, and are therefore key to putting a 'spring in your step'. Aside from assisting with a wide range of movement, they also contribute to stabilising the legs and feet.

So, take a moment to experience your ankles right now. See how they work. Lift them up, flex and point them, see how far they twist inwards and outwards. Notice how the muscles of your legs turn on as you perform each of these movements. How fluid or stiff do your ankles feel? Is there any fluid build up? Could you benefit from putting your ankles up against a wall? Feel the bones and ligaments surrounding them, and say a little thank you for the mobility and direction that they allow your feet to experience.

Your *ability to create and change direction stems* from your ankles, and this ability in and of itself needs to be acknowledged as a true blessing.

As you show gratitude to your ankles, recognise that through them you have been given the ability to plant your feet, or to lift away from a certain spot and change direction as often as you like, both throughout the day and within your life. The ankles represent your ability to do this in your personal life. If you're not happy with your life situation as it currently is, know that your ankles will support your need to change course.

The ankles, therefore, are a part of your body that requires protection and care. Whenever a change in life direction shows up—whether it's in your personal life, your career or your romantic life—pay special attention to your ankles. Send them loving energy and support; perhaps consider housing them in more ankle-supportive shoes.

Perhaps even an ankle bracelet could be worn, as a symbolical reminder that your new direction is blessed. A little self-massage with a granular scrub or body lotion is also a brilliant way to care for your ankles, as it helps to relax the numerous tendons and ligaments in the ankle region, therefore assisting to prevent strain and injury to the area.

If you're currently finding it difficult to work out which direction to choose, go into your garden, or to a place in nature that you love, and focus your attention on your heart area. Breathe in and out deeply and slowly—you want to slow yourself down—three times. Clear your mind, close your eyes (as this brings you deeper into yourself) and ask the question about your direction with your bare feet firmly planted on the ground.

Which direction feels right? Ask your question and see how your body responds. Pay particular attention to the emotions that surface, as your emotions are the language of the soul. It is therefore essential that you express them regularly, instead of suppressing them with addictive substances: food, alcohol, workaholism or distraction.

Your emotions are constantly indicating the direction your soul wishes to go. If the response to your question makes you feel expansive, light and excited then the universe supports the direction in which you wish to head. You can move forward with certainty and confidence. If, on the other hand, your body and your energy feels heavy, constricted or flat then the universe will not support this path and you will constantly experience struggle, frustration and resistance, no matter how hard you try to make things work. Essentially, you'll be going against 'the flow' by choosing an unsupported path. This may all sound a little airy-fairy, however, think about the times you've tried to take on any task or project with flat energy. It was an effort; a struggle, and you hated everything about it. Now, think about a time that you had something to do that you really loved. Even if things were difficult, you saw the obstacles as challenges, rather than a reason to stop. In fact, you enjoyed the challenges and grew from the experience. That's the difference. Always tap into your body for an answer; it will speak very loudly and very clearly if you just slow yourself down, centre yourself and take a moment to listen.

> *This is the key difference between listening to your head and listening to your heart.*

One way provides the answers that society and family programming offer, and comes from external sources or past experiences, and the other way provides messages that form the key to your heart and happiness, and come from within and from the present moment. The choice therefore is quite simple; it's just a case of having the courage to follow the correct path. Your ankles' flexibility and strength rest upon your commitment to take the time and ensure you are making the right decisions, and therefore head in the right direction, according to your heart's needs.

Remember to do this gratitude exercise daily, or at the very least when you're at a crossroads in life. Your ankles, feet and toes support your entire body weight, so you must ensure that they are supporting you to manifest a path that is in keeping with your heart's journey.

SHOES

So now that we've paid special attention to the ankles, feet and toes let's celebrate them with some beautiful shoes.

Your shoes add embellishment to your overall outfit. They tell the story or set the tone for your entire ensemble. Whether you're feeling casual—requiring a flatter shoe, sexy—a stiletto, formal or smart casual—pumps, or sporty and active—canvas shoes.

It is therefore important to have a number of smart staples in your shoe closet that allow you to truly express who you want to be. Having the following 10 sets of shoes will enable you to be prepared for all occasions and every season. If you then want to build from here, that's perfectly fine. But, start with these basics and you'll never get caught out and will always have the right shoe for every outfit. Regardless of your mood, there will be a pair of shoes that will enhance and house your beautiful feet and ankles.

Now, lovingly, select your perfect pair.

Here is a list of the top 10 shoes that every woman should have in her wardrobe, in order to be prepared for any occasion and every mood, that will also cover you for both warmer and colder climates.

1. Black Pumps

This classic pair of heels is basic, however they also scream sexy. Black pumps can be worn at the office, to a formal function and around town. They can be dressed up or down according to your mood and the occasion. Your pumps can be any variation of a closed-toe shoe, with a heel. It is up to you to choose the height and thickness of the heel for your pump. As these shoes are *the most versatile pair*, it is important to invest in the best quality you can afford.

1b) Nude Pumps

Having a second pair of pumps allows you to utilise more of your wardrobe. More of the tans, browns and navy colours in your wardrobe can be worn with nude pumps. You'll also find they have a sliming and lengthening effect on your legs, as the nude colour works to create the illusion of being an extension of your leg.

2. Sling backs

These shoes are a great summer alternative to the classic pump. They serve a similar function and are just as effective and stylish, only they're more suitable for warmer climates.

⌇⋇ Feet, Ankles & Shoes ⋇⌇

3. Casual Sandals

Casual sandals include anything that you enjoy running around in on a very hot day. They include flip flops (thongs) that you can wear at the beach, and anything else that you can throw on easily. These can be as fancy or as low key as you wish, but they are an absolute must in any wardrobe, as they can pair with most of the casual pieces in your summer wardrobe.

4. Dressy sandals

These are sandals that may have a central bar through the front of the shoe or may go straight across. Whether you choose sandals with a heel or a wedge, cork shoes or flats, doesn't matter. As long as you have a pair of shoes that you can throw on with a pretty summer dress. Dressy sandals come in many different shapes and sizes, however they do not fit into the category of something you could wear to the beach. They can also function as an alternative pair of going-out shoes, and are often more comfortable than stilettos.

5. Ballet Flats

These shoes are brilliant for running around in, whilst remaining stylish, and they come in a wide array of colours. Ballet flats allow you to throw on a pop of colour or texture, while still remaining comfortable.

6. Peep Toe Shoes

These shoes are a great for summer. A variation of the dressy sandal, they allow you to show off your newly pedicured toes. They look great with denim, as well as with a summer dress. Very Marilyn Munroe, and therefore timeless.

6. Wedge Shoes

A more comfortable and versatile version of your standard high heel ... and so much more fun, too. They look great with your sundress or with casual shorts. They also go well with jeans and pants.

7. Women's ankle boots

A casual boot that can be worn with skirts and jeans. Heel height and thickness are your own preference, however it is always best to start out with a neutral colour, and then expand your shoe-collection colours once you've established your basic wardrobe.

8. **Leather Boots**

A pair of long winter boots that either extend to the knee or above it, are an essential item in any wardrobe. Best to choose a neutral colour to begin with, so that you can wear your boots with pretty much any of the items in your winter wardrobe.

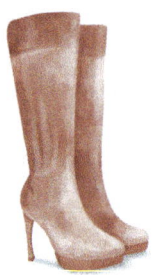  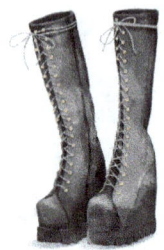

9. **Canvas Sneakers**

These are similar to ballet flats in their usability, however they promote a more casual look. Shop for a good quality sole and a slip-on type canvas sneaker to wear with your casual outfits.

Optional, yet often essential, extra options:

Wet weather boots e.g. gumboots

Gym shoes e.g. trainers

NOTE: Once you have built your basic shoe collection it is important to look for additional textures and prints, to add interest and variety to your shoe collection. Look for shoes with metallic finishes, animal prints or snakeskin texture. These will all add an interest and pop factor to your feet.

BODY AWARENESS EXERCISE

> *Beginning the process of acknowledging your body's amazingness*

Now that we've looked at our feet, ankles, and shoes, I'd like to change focus for a moment. This exercise can be used for any body part you have issues with … Let me guide you through an exercise that I feel may bring you to a deeper level of appreciation for the one and only body you were given, and the only one you will ever have. It is very important therefore, to work with your body, rather than against it.

Appreciation is a loving place from which to start honouring your whole self, giving you a brand new sense of perspective on you.

All criticism, complaints and comparisons need to be pushed aside during this process. If you look for something that's wrong with yourself, then believe me, you'll find it. Your mind will become trained to look out for the negative, and our brains are already wired in that direction. So, it's now time to retrain the way you view yourself. Essentially, it's time to change the channel.

If you are currently unhappy with what you see in the mirror, the most powerful way to shift this negative mindset towards yourself is to give gratitude for what you have. *Give gratitude for the miracle of the human body that you are fortunate enough to possess. Give thanks for the tireless unacknowledged work your body does for you every single moment of your life.*

People work from one of two places: either they work from the arena of fear—which comprises of attacking the self and is heavily ego dependent—or they work from the arena of love—gratitude and appreciation are qualities of love. What I am asking you to develop here, therefore, is a shift towards the quality of love and a shift away from the self-attacking state of fear. Love what you were given, because it is yours and yours alone. There is no double up.

Even if you are currently standing in front of the mirror hating what you see, remind yourself that this is coming from a state of fear that you have the capacity to replace with love. You may initially experience resistance in these exercises, but I recommend sticking with them until you feel a shift. Remember that each new skill set you acquire requires practice. To embody a new skill set you must repeat it 300 times; to master it you must repeat the exercise 3,000 times. Essentially, I'm saying that it might take close to a year before you let your resistance down and actually allow yourself to express true love for yourself. That's fine. It's worth the time and effort.

Just remember that *true beauty can only come through love*, and true love can only come through authentic connection. You have, no doubt, experienced moments of this connection with loved ones—where you are truly engaged and present, and you wanted to do loving things for them. Whether it's a loved one, a small child or a puppy, or it could even be a project, or something as simple as cooking or gardening. You have experienced connection with something or someone at one time or another. And this connection is beautiful. You were completely present with them or it at the time. You fully gave your self to them. You came alive, your eyes and face lit up, you became more expansive and more open to possibility. All of you was there in that moment. You didn't care about what others thought, because you were lost in that moment. Your sense of connectedness in that moment is the true expression of self. It is the expression of love. And it is also the embodiment of beauty.

What I'm about to ask you to do here, is to try and gain that experience of connection that you've felt with others or with projects—that filled you up and made you come alive—and funnel that energy onto your *self*. Make yourself the study of this project. Make yourself the object that piques your curiosity. Make yourself the thing you get lost in and fall in love with. Feel awe when you look at and look into yourself. Make it your ambition to find the beauty within you and all around you.

I will be giving you practical tips on how to enhance each area of your body along the way, but what really matters to the entirety of this endeavour is gaining a solid connection with, and an appreciation of, yourself.

> *Experiencing connection, love and appreciation for your <u>self</u> the only logical way to view yourself, and is paramount in treating yourself in a loving way. This is what I call truly beautiful.*

Chapter 2

Legs, The Golden Ratio & Hosiery

THE LEGS

Let's now move up to the legs. What do you see? What do you feel? Really feel into your legs right now and gaze over these miracles of nature. Start just above your ankles, at the base of your shins. Notice the skin that holds various muscles in place. Is your skin smooth, rough, flaky? Is it irritated in patches? What colour is your skin? Run your fingers over the skin on your legs and feel the sensation. These legs are constantly moving you around.

Now that you're paying attention, can you feel the blood pumping through them? Would you say your blood circulation is healthy or poor? Can you feel the lymphatic fluid that pumps through them? Inactivity can cause poor circulation of the blood or body fluids. Could you be in need of a brisk walk? By the same token, extended periods of standing can also lead to fluid retention, so it could be a case of needing to raise your legs and give them a rest.

How about the muscles in your legs? Are there any particularly tight or sore muscles?

Your leg muscles are divided into different sections as far as function goes. The hamstring muscles form the muscle group you see on the back of your thigh. Their job is essentially to allow the knees to bend.

At the front of the upper legs you have a group of muscles called the quadriceps that allow the knees to straighten from a bent position. Essentially, they help you to get up.

Then you have your inner thigh muscles—called adductors—that are switched on when you do things such as riding a horse.

Then you have your knees. Whenever, I'm at yoga I hear teachers talk about the need to respect the knees. These are the largest joints in your body, and they connect the upper leg and the lower leg. Aside from bearing the weight of your upper body, they enable the legs to walk, run, jump, kick, twist and turn.

Finally, we have the lower leg muscles that extend from the knee to the ankle. These are known as the calf, the back of the lower legs, and the peroneus muscles, sitting on the front of the lower leg. (Their function was explained in the ankle section.)

Where are your legs feeling tight? At the front of the legs? At the backs of the legs? Around the knee joint? Around the shins? Around the hips or butt? Taking time to pay attention to these subtle nuances will help you to become more aware of your body, and, more importantly, how you may be contributing to your own unease.

Your legs are more than mere appendages. Your legs carry you through your life on a daily basis. Your legs are your very own self-support system, keeping you upright. They're also the main contributors in creating motion, enabling you to get from point A to point B more effectively than any other part of the body. They allow you to stand firm, to walk tall and to stride with pride. Bending at the knees allows you to stand up and sit down, to go from standing to sitting or walking, or from kicking to dancing, in a heartbeat.

You can amble, walk briskly or bolt through life. It's your choice. Your legs will help you achieve all of these states. Appreciate them for this incredible ability.

Whether your legs are 'too short' or 'too long', 'too fat' or 'too thin', try to find gratitude in your heart for their ability to support you and transport you forward in your life, to wherever it is that you wish to go. Imagine, for a moment, what it would be like if you didn't have them.

Today, when you look at your legs, make the decision to use them to move forward confidently, with faith and pride that you're on the right path for you.

Dedicate some time to thinking about how you could appreciate your legs and show them more love. A body scrub before or during your shower, maybe? The application of body butter or oil after each shower. A gentle walk, some martial arts training to strengthen them, some stretching exercises such as yoga, to ensure that they stay strong yet supple, and to ensure ease of movement.

Just tap in and connect with what it is your legs would like to experience. They will tell you that they want to move forward with ease and grace, not stiffness and pain. Think of all the ways you can enhance their mobility.

Now that you've given your legs a little more attention and gratitude, it is time to flatter them with the following information about the golden ratio and how it applies to fashion.

THE GOLDEN RATIO

What is the golden ratio, you might ask?

The golden ratio is a recurring mathematical formula that is found throughout nature, bringing about a sense of order and coherence. When applied to fashion, it can give the illusion of having longer legs. So, how do you apply this rule to your legs? Simply take out a tape measure and measure yourself from the floor to your shoulders. (For the most precise measurement, ensure that you are measuring yourself in the pair of shoes that you intend to wear with the skirt that you intend to wear, etc.)

Once you have the measurement from the floor to your shoulders, you then divide this number by 1.618, which is the golden ratio number.

Let's give an example of the measurement, where the number from floor to shoulder is 150cm. In this example you will end up with a measurement of 92.7cm. The 150cm measurement from floor to shoulder, divided by 1.618 (the golden ratio) equals 92.7cm.

This number (92.7cm) is your ideal hem length for dresses, skirts and shorts, when you're wearing this pair of shoes.

The number obviously changes with different sets of shoes, as the ratio depends on height. For example, according to the golden ratio, it will suit you better to wear a shorter skirt with flat shoes than you would with heels.

So, now that you know your ideal hem length to show off your legs, let's get those legs into some leg-hugging hosiery options.

Go on, show them off!

LEGGINGS AND HOSIERY

When it comes to hosiery, there are certain items that you really want to keep in stock, especially if you have an office job.

1. **Pantyhose in nude, tan or black**.

By pantyhose, I'm talking about sheer 10–25 denier yam. It is a breathable material and is therefore great for wear during the summer seasons. Pantyhose work to cover any imperfections on the skin, as well as providing a mild level of body shape wear for the legs. Pantyhose worn under a skirt gives your look a more professional edge.

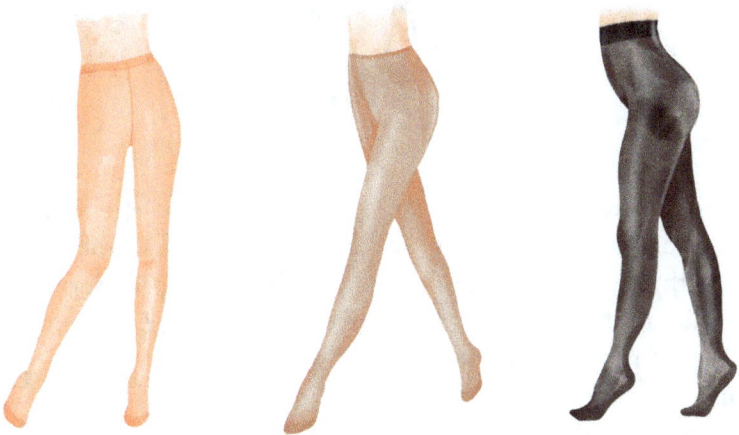

Pantyhose, however, are a choice and not the rule. If you have beautiful legs and great skin, all the more reason to show them off and wear them bare. Some women like the added help of a tan that pantyhose offer, however, with the advent of tanning lotion pantyhose is not always such a necessity.

Finally, you do *not* want to wear pantyhose with open-toed shoes as this looks extremely dated, as well as generally awkward.

The next essential hosiery item is:

2. Opaque tights

Opaque tights are a thicker denier yarn than pantyhose, and do not allow people to see any part of the leg under them, other than the shape of your leg. Being thicker, they are also warmer. Therefore, they serve as more of a colder-climate hosiery item. Don't feel like waxing or shaving your legs in winter? No problem … nobody will see or know any better, unless you tell them.

Opaque tights work really well under winter skirts and loose tunics, as well as beneath any long tops or shirts that cover the backside. They also look great with over-the-knee boots.

If you're ever on the fence about wearing a particular skirt or dress because you think it may be too short, remember that you can generally pull off a shorter hem length when wearing opaque tights, as no skin is being revealed.

It is best to get your first pair of opaque tights in black, as they are more versatile than any other colour. Then, feel free to build your collection.

3. **Black leggings** are the next essential item I recommend.

They can be pleggings (faux leather)

or black jeggings (jean material leggings)

or simply a cotton legging.

Leggings can be worn best in a similar way to opaque tights. Just remember the rule of balancing out tight with loose. If you're wearing something tight on your legs, then you want a looser, more comfortable top half of the body.

Leggings are easy to wear and are made of a thicker material than opaque tights. They're great with boots, a loose, longer top, and a scarf.

3. Cotton socks

Cotton socks in skin colour and black. If you don't own socks, you're going to suffer a wardrobe malfunction at some stage, unless you're prepared to live your life in sandals and flip flops. The aim of socks is to create a smooth transition from pant to shoe, and they also work to elongate the leg. Aside from this, as cotton is a natural fibre it allows the feet to breathe within the shoe, causing less foot odour and blisters, caused by feet rubbing against the inside of closed-in shoes.

Once these staples are in place, you can start building more fun pairs of lace and patterned or coloured socks, to add a little fun to your legs.

4. Patterned stockings

Patterned stockings can work in your favour if you want to make your legs look slimmer. Choose a pair of stockings that have a vertical pattern on them to create this effect.

If, however, you carry most of your weight in your upper torso, or have wider shoulders, you can draw attention downwards by wearing bold, colourful and larger-print designs on your legs.

So, step forward with confidence and a sense of excitement, now that you've created your hosiery collection.

Chapter 3
A Brief Introduction to Body Types

Below is a very brief explanation of different body types. I don't want you to feel that you need to be pigeonholed into a specific body type or that one shape is better than another. The human form is always made up of a combination of curves and lines. Some are curvier in certain sections of their body, and some are straighter. All are beautiful, and it is only when we embrace our body type and wear styles that flatter our shapes that we will really sparkle. It's pointless wanting to be less curvy or curvier in certain parts of your body when you are not. And all the weight loss in the world won't make you an hourglass shape if you are a natural H shape. So please take the time to look at your silhouette and really pay attention to your bust, waist, and hips. Make a mental note of whether your figure has more curves or straighter lines in each of these areas. Or is it a combination of curvy and straight? Wherever there is outward curvature, you may want to apply less detail or bulk in your garments. Where there are straighter lines or areas of the body that are proportionally less bulky, feel free to add zips, bows, frills, buttons and so on.

Not everyone is a definite fit to one of the body types I am about to explain. Some are a combination of two body types. This is very important to remember. I have often seen women who are a combination of an A shape with larger bust or a V shape with an H shape waist. Bear this in mind while you are looking through this chapter and adjust accordingly. Ultimately, when it comes to fashion, though, it's about creating balance and harmony stylistically.

This is purely a reference guide, so that you will be able to understand what I am talking about when I say things like "H/rectangular shape",

"V or triangle shape," and so on. As you read through the book, I will go into a lot more detail on how to best enhance each shape and what to avoid. For now, however, let me introduce you to five of the most common body shapes:

Rectangular/ H Shape

This shape has very little in the way of a defined waist—very few curves—and is often a more athletic build.

Your main aim with clothing will be to visually break up the body by layering or to mimic your current figure with straighter lines in your clothing or pattern/print choices. Shift dresses and pants with a false waistline (either empire line or dropped waist styles) help to enhance this body shape.

O-Shape/Oval Shape

This body shape tends to accumulate most of its weight on the belly and waist, where the tummy is wider than the bust outline.

The focus with this body type is to minimize attention to the belly and accentuate the legs, wrists and décolleté. Fabrics that drape and don't cling around the mid-section are ideal. Curvier hemlines and fluid tunics or flowy, longer styled outwear/cardigans are ideal for this body type.

The Hourglass Figure

An hourglass has a smaller waist balanced out with fuller bust and hips (that are approximately the same size). This creates a very curvaceous and balanced feminine silhouette.

For best results wear clothing that accentuates your already curvaceous body. Your figure is enhanced by drawing attention to your small waist with a belt, for example.

Triangle/A Shape

People with this body shape tend to gain their weight on their hips, thighs, and buttocks. You may also have a smaller bust and narrow shoulders, as well as a well-defined waist.

Adding volume and detail around the shoulders and neckline will help draw people's attention away from the hips and thighs.

Inverted Triangular

This shape often has hips that are narrower than the shoulders, little to middling waist definition and tends to be more athletic in build. Weight gain normally occurs through the torso, bust/shoulders and back area.

Focus your attention downwards towards your hips, with the aim of creating a fuller and rounder hip and thigh area. Wider palazzo pant styles and tiered or A-style skirts will help to balance out this shape.

Now for edits required for Chapter 4. Page 52 the first line or point all the words are running together. Please fix this So that it reads : 1. Think of all the things you have to look forward to in the future. As well as how you wish to move forward on each of these goals. Write them down.

Chapter 4

Thighs, Hips and Buttocks; Skirts, Pants and Jeans

THE THIGHS

The thighs are one area of the body that receives the most loathing and criticism. Yet how much time is spent acknowledging and appreciating the role of your thighs?

Your thighs are the powerhouse of your body. Without the strength of those concentrated muscles, all working together in perfect unison, you wouldn't be moving forward very easily in life.

It's hard to look at the thighs in isolation, as they are attached to the hips and the pelvis, which give you your thrust power in life. They're also attached to your knees, which carry a major load and act as the shock absorbers of your body.

Your thighs are, therefore, smack bang in between your body's ability to propel yourself forward and its ability to bear the load of what is necessary to move you forward in life.

The upper legs are commonly known as the thighs and are one of the strongest groups of muscles of the body, connected to two of our major joints—the hips and the knees.

Join any martial arts training class and you will be told often that if presented with a situation where you will need to defend yourself, you should focus on using your hips and thighs, because this is where a woman's

Thighs, Hips and Buttocks; Skirts, Pants and Jeans

greatest physical power lies. 'Kick and run!' is the general advice for women. Both require strong thighs.

The better your relationship with your thighs—the healthier, firmer, and more switched on the muscles are—the easier it will be to move forward in the direction of your desired outcome.

If all your thigh muscles are properly engaged, then your knees, hips and lower back will be able to perform their functions more effectively and with a lot less pain, as well as a lot less wear and tear.

The thighs are made up of muscles that sit under the hips, pelvis and buttocks, and insert into the knees. They are divided into three main groups: the quadriceps—front thigh muscles, the hamstrings—back thigh muscles, and the hip adductors—inner thigh muscles.

The purpose of the front of the thighs—the quadriceps—is to extend the knee and flex the hip. Think of kicking your leg straight from a bent position.

Just try this movement now. Really tense up all the front thigh muscles as you kick your leg straight from a bent position. You can feel the main muscles that are turned on are the muscles at the front and side of the upper leg.

If you bring your knee up towards your hip you are creating a hip flexion movement.

Feeling disempowered? Your quads are teaming with power! Sign up to a martial arts or kickboxing class and see what you're made of.

The back of the thighs—the hamstrings—are required for knee flexion and hip extension.

Knee flexion is better known as bending your knees. Bend your knee really slowly so that you can feel your hamstring muscles doing their thing.

Knee flexion

Hip extension is when you move your upper leg backwards. Lift your leg backwards and feel your hamstrings contract.

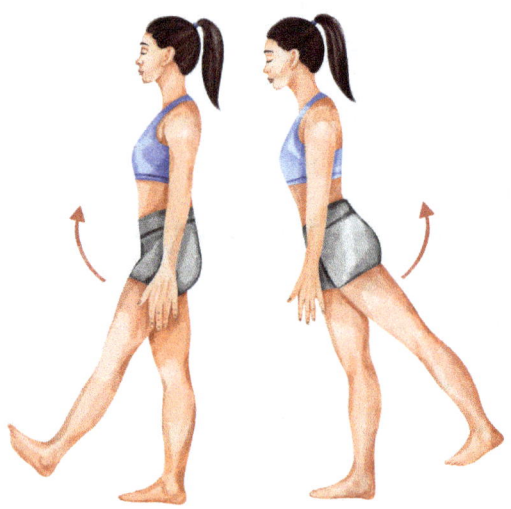

Both of the above actions—bending your knee and extending your thigh and hip—are integral to helping you do things such as jumping, running and walking, especially if you want to jump higher or run faster.

> *Your thighs, therefore, are like your body's catapult, propelling you towards your desired destination.*

Think *freedom* as you use your hamstrings. Think about moving towards your goals with greater *speed*.

And the inner thighs muscles—hip adductors—bring the thighs in towards the centre of the body.

Imagine squeezing your thighs together. Think of all the ways you use this movement. Riding a horse or bike.

Hip adductors also help stabilise the body when you're playing sports that require you to shift quickly from one direction to the next, such as soccer or hip-hop dancing.

The hip adductor muscles help to *stabilise* your hips. If your inner thigh muscles are working properly then your knees will love you for it. Especially if you're a runner.

The other thing that strong inner thigh muscles help with is the internal rotation of the leg —twisting the leg inwards. This is important because your outer thighs create the outward rotation of your knees. So strong inner thighs will provide counterbalance, keeping your knees tracking properly.

The inner thighs, therefore, are responsible for keeping everything *on track*. Your hips, lower back and knees will love you when your inner thighs are functioning well. They create the *stability* that all your activities require in order to continue working effectively over the long term.

So, let's summarise what the thighs do when they're switched on, or in action:

- Our thighs provide us with incredible *power* (quads). Think of the force in a kick.
- They offer us a great sense of *freedom* as they propel us towards our goal with an explosive and *accelerated* pace (hamstrings). Think of their role in helping us run, jump and walk.
- Our thighs also ensure the *stability* of our core and lower body (hip adductors). Strong inner thigh muscles *keep everything on track* by ensuring healthier knees, hips and lower back.

When we're at rest—sitting down—the thighs create what is commonly known as your lap.

When you're in a state of peace and trust the process of life, things can often just 'fall into your lap'.

Meditate on what has occurred for you recently that you didn't really have to make any effort or stride towards. It just came to you and fell into your lap.

The reason? When you're too focused on controlling all outcomes, you're only focusing on productivity and not allowing the process to unfold naturally. Hard work alone doesn't guarantee results. It requires a healthy dose of faith also. This is often the missing link. Instead of *pushing* everything into eventuating, why not try *allowing*?

Be in the moment and focus on each step of the process—step by step, as the moment unfolds. Once this has been done, let go! Relax! Take a break! Know that it is now in the 'laps of the Gods'. Too much focus on outcome will only lead to frustration, misery and a lot of stiffness and pain in the body.

Another thing to consider when seated in this position is what is it that you do allow into your lap? Your thighs, at rest, create a cushion or resting space for things you hold dear.

Is it a great book? A craft project? Your kitten? A small child?

Both the active and passive states of your thighs are equally important. Learn to love your thighs, at rest and in action.

Recognise how powerful, dynamic and stabilising they are when you're active, and how comforting they can be in repose.

Either of these states enables you to bring what you love into your life. Spend your time working out exactly what that might be.

Take action, definitely, but remember to also take rest. Both states are equally powerful when your mind is focused on your present. An important aspect of this is the ability to move between both states. Either way, remember that your thighs are there to support you.

Now that you've taken the time to acknowledge the incredible role your thighs play, and how essential they are in enabling you to move forward with strength, agility and stability, how could you appreciate your thighs a little more?

Remember that your thighs are there to help you move your knees and hips. Is there a restlessness that needs to be expressed through dance, sport, running or swimming? Do you want to kick something? A ball or a padded cushion is probably the best and safest place to start!

Could you take your thighs for a walk? Have you missed the joy of jumping a skipping rope? Or do you just need to take your thighs to the gym and celebrate their strength and power?

Have you been too active? Do you now need to appreciate your thighs in their relaxed state? Do they need a good stretch? Could you benefit from sitting in meditation? Or do you just want to rest and let somebody else take over? Sit down and enjoy the things that calm you. It could be patting your dog, reading your favourite book, writing, or reading a book to your child. Whatever brings you the most joy and relaxation.

By focusing your attention on what you could do for your thighs, you begin to enter a completely different headspace. Instead of seeing them as a site of dissatisfaction, you're finally celebrating your thighs for the miracles they perform.

Only once you can appreciate the magnificent role your thighs play, and the incredible structure they really are, then and only then is it possible to look at ways of physically enhancing your thighs with clothing.

An Exercise

For this section—about hips, thighs and buttocks—I want you to do some writing. The act of writing itself, helps you connect with the subconscious part of you, that you wouldn't normally connect with on a day to day basis.

Unless you're a seasoned meditator or have some way of connecting inward, the subconscious mind is often unheard. Most of your breakthroughs or ah-hah moments come when you take the time to connect inwards. By taking the time to answer these questions, and through putting pen to paper, you'll be able to connect with the underlying magnificence of these areas of your body, and the role they play in your life.

Answering the following set of questions is a great way to connect with the inherent qualities of each of these areas of your body, areas that you may not be appreciating because you've spent too much time focusing on superficial aspects such as the visual form of your thighs.

So, get your pen ready and let's begin!

- Where is your power? Somewhere in your life, you feel empowered. Somewhere in your life you have strength. Is it in the physical, financial, family, social, romantic, educational, career or spiritual aspect of your life?

- Are you naturally gifted in one specific area? Do people come to you for something in particular? Do you have a natural flair when it comes to cooking, to meeting new people, to dancing or to getting people together?

- What propels you forward? What inspires you? It really doesn't matter what it is. It just matters that you know what you love doing, and you do it naturally, without any encouragement from others.

- What gives you that extra injection? Once you've done that thing—going for a run before your workday, hosting a dinner party, playing your guitar, finishing an extra book on your favourite topic, finalising a work report to a level that you're proud of, going to church, meditating—you come alive. It holds your interest without anybody else telling you to do it. Focus on what these activities are for you. Become hyperaware of them, and how you feel in these moments. If you can harness the ability to hold onto this state when you find yourself in a moment of weakness, you'll discover solutions to problems that you never would have found if you were in a low mood.

- What could you be doing at an accelerated rate? Have you slowed down in an area where you need to speed up? What will it take to propel you forward?

- Where is the stability in your life? Think of the areas in your life that are on track. Is it your family? Work? Friendships? Church? Spiritual Life? Financial foundations?

- What measures do you have in place to keep you stable during difficult moments?

- What do you need in order to keep yourself on track? Is there a part of you that's weak, that needs to be strengthened in order to give you the ability to move forward with confidence in a sustainable way?

The more you put into answering these questions, the more you'll get out of what your body has the ability to teach you.

The thighs often loom large as the bane of women's existence. However, once you can embrace them, suddenly, they becomes a part of you to be viewed with pride. My hope is that you've now established a deeper respect for this area of your body.

From this revised vantage point, I want you to take a closer, and a more appreciative look at your thighs.

Go and stand in front of your mirror and really look at this area ... *without judgement.*Simply observe!

- Are your thighs muscular?
- Are they more pillowy?
- Or are they a combination of both?
- Is the texture of the skin in this area smooth or rough?
- Is the skin tone an even colour?
- Are your thighs rounder or more straight up and down?
- Are your thighs the widest point of your body?
- Are your hip and thigh measurements quite similar?

Note this down because we will be using these notes to help you in your figure enhancing styling routine.

THE HIPS

Moving up a little further now to the region of the hips.

The hip joint is the point at which your legs are joined to the trunk of your body.

Whether you're standing still or moving around it is the hips that support the weight of your upper body. In other words, the hips are responsible for *holding you up*.

It is therefore clear that the hips form a foundational base for your body. Stability and the ability to trust life to unfold in a way that's right for you comes from the hips.

By the same token they give the lower body *thrust power, range of movement* and they work as *shock absorbers* for all the different movements of the upper legs.

You can observe how your hips work by placing your hands on your hips and then pushing your hips forwards and backwards. Think of riding a horse and the back and forward motion that occurs. It's the ball and socket joint of the hip that allows for this gliding motion to happen within the joint.

Now, stand on one leg and bring the other leg out and away from your body. You'll notice that your leg can extend forwards, backwards, sideways. It can go in towards your body (adduction) and away from your body (abduction).

Think of a graceful ballerina with her legs extending back, forwards, sideways, squatting in plié, rotating her legs. It's the hip joint that enables these movements to occur with relative ease.

Your hip joint also allows you to twist your leg inwards (internal rotation) and outwards (external rotation).

Your hip joint is especially effective when you are performing exercises such as lunges, squats, running, walking, jumping, climbing stairs. Essentially, the hips are responsible for all the movements of the upper leg—obviously in conjunction with your thighs and butt.

Your hips also absorb a lot of the shock that would come from running, jumping, squatting and lunging movements. When the hips are balanced it becomes easier to progress forward with enthusiasm and passion. However, when the hips are out of alignment everything becomes harder because the focus will be on pain rather than progress.

So, it is now time to check your hips. I want you to feel into the sensations of the hips as well as all the muscles you can feel around them.

Simply close your eyes and breathe in and out a few times. Send your awareness down to your hips and feel into any sensations you may be experiencing in this area. You may feel stiffness, tingling, heat, cold, tenderness or nothing at all. Whatever it is just acknowledge the feeling. Don't judge it, just observe it.

Once you recognise the sensation, check in to see if this sensation has an emotion attached to it. For example, the stiffness might be tied to a feeling of frustration or resistance to moving forward, perhaps even the feeling that there is nothing to move forward to. It could even be a fear of standing on your own two feet (without anyone beside you).

The heat or tingling could be related to an emotion of excitement or overdoing things. And if you're experiencing sensations of cold it could be linked to feelings of lack of enthusiasm or of not trusting your current direction.

> NB. The above are examples not specifics—the emotion you attach to your sensation is entirely your own. I am simply illustrating potential examples of connections of sensations and feelings. However, everyone has their own unique set of emotions, so I want to clarify that these are purely examples.

Once you've explored the feelings related to your hips, it's time to ask yourself the following questions.

Exercise

Empowering your hips:

1. Think of all the things you have to look forward to in the future. As well as how you wish to move forward on each of these goals. Write them down.

2. Think of all the ways you have been able to stand on your own two feet and support yourself. Also, look at all the areas in your life where you feel supported. Write these down.

3. Think of all the times that it was easy to make progress in your life. In which areas of your life have you moved forward with ease?

4. Where is your life in balance/aligned? Is it with family, friends, at work, with finances, romance, spiritually, intellectually? Wherever you have balance in your life make a note of it. Try and work out what your attitude is in these areas, what internal dialogue you have around these areas of your life and where within your body you feel this balance and harmony. Is the feeling one of lightness, is it a colour, or a shape? Whatever comes to mind when you think of an area of your life that feels balanced write down all the details around how you feel. This can become your success template. What is to stop you from adapting your success template attitudes, behaviours and expectations to the areas of your life that aren't in balance?

5. Where do you feel a sense of freedom of movement or expression? Is it with your family, your friends, with your partner, your work, your hobbies? Finding your freedom of movement will speak volumes about what matters to you. Knowing what really matters to you in life will propel you forward and onward at record speed, in a way that oozes ease and grace.

6. Where in your life are you feeling FREE? Write these down.

Now, where in your life would you like to feel more freedom? You were born free! You may be holding onto emotions and self-limiting beliefs that are holding you back. Itemise all the things you are HOLDING onto and LET THEM GO! Write down all the things you need to stop holding onto and imagine a campfire. Rip up your list and, item by item, throw it into the flames from your hip joint.

If you can appreciate and recognise your hips for the mobilising potential they possess, you probably wouldn't ever bend from the waist to pick something up ever again. You would bend at the knees and use the thrust power of your hips to pick up the actual item. Your hips are your power reservoirs. Need to perform explosive movements such as sprints, squats or leaps? Then look no further than your hips. Once your hips are working properly you'll find that the rest of the body will work a lot better too.

Remember that your hips, regardless of how wide or narrow they may be, are providing you with the thrust power to move you forward in life. They also determine the pace at which your body moves.

With this understanding in mind, if you need to slow down the pace or, contrarily, if you require a kick start to get you moving toward a particular idea or project, then take the time to feel and breath into your hip area.

Physically, if you're feeling this area of your life could do with a shakeup, then that is literally what you should do ... give your hips, a little shake, a little shimmy. Look into belly dancing, salsa or samba to get your hips working. Alternately, your hips may require a good stretch with yoga or a tai chi routine, because you've been moving too fast or too much and now you need to slow down and take some time to consciously connect.

Whatever they require, pay close attention to what your hips are saying and give them the appreciation and respect they deserve.

If I can now ask you to take a look at your hips:

> Rest your attention on these boney structures.
> Check to see whether one side feels tighter than the other.
> Are you feeling stable across this section of your body?
> Does one hip sit higher than the other?
> Do you have hips that sit higher or lower on your body?
> Simply note down these observations.

At the level of fashion your hips matter too, as they dictate the best length of your tops, blouses and jackets. As mentioned earlier, the legs are connected to the trunk via the hip joint, so it is interesting to see how bringing a blouse or jacket to the level of the hips or below it can affect the overall impact of your outfit.

If you believe that pulling your top down to cover up the wider section of your thighs and butt will hide this area, you need to realise that you're actually drawing attention *to* this area instead. Whatever you resist persists, as they say.

A person's eye will always travel to the end point of a piece of clothing (i.e. the end of your top), so pulling your tops down will only cause the eye to travel to the wider part of your hips and thighs.

Furthermore, if you are petite, you'll find that pulling tops down makes you appear shorter. As your leg length will be cut visually across the thighs, this will cause them to appear shorter than they really are.

Rotating your hips forward and then pulling up from the abdomen to lengthen your spine is the starting point for a taller silhouette, as well as better posture.

Couple great posture with ending your tops and jackets at the perfect spot and you'll be on your way to a more balanced and harmonious looking frame.

In general, the best place to end tops and jackets is at the hip bone. By doing this you are displaying the full leg. The only time you would want to wear longer tops is when your legs are longer than your torso.

Note that the top ends at (or around) the hipbone, providing balance and harmony to the upper and lower regions of the body.

THE BUTTOCKS

Moving around now to the buttocks. Back up to the mirror and take a long look at what you've been blessed with in this region.

What messages are you communicating with yourself about this area when you look in the mirror? Are these messages beneficial or hurtful? Try being kind and uplifting.

Look at the roundness of your very own mobile set of cushions. Is your butt round and perky? Is it lower and hanging? Is it flatter or rounder? If you can identify the type of derrière you possess it will be easier for you when it comes to selecting figure enhancing pants and jeans, and even more comfortably fitting underwear.

Why do we even need buttocks?

Well for one ... they protect the lower spine from friction whenever you're sitting down. Your butt enables you to take the pressure off your feet when you're not standing ... *however*, if you sit down too much you end up with a case of numb bum.

It may sound funny and silly but if you find yourself sitting down too much, for example in front of a computer screen all day, you can easily send your butt muscles to sleep. And that's not a good thing.

The muscles of the backside—called the gluteal muscles—are the strongest muscles in the human body and are responsible for the movement of your hips and thighs. They help you to pull your thighs behind you when you walk, they help your hips to move the leg towards your midline and they also help rotate your hips inwards and outwards so that you can perform your greatest happy dance! Without these muscles how would we ever perform the infamous chicken dance at family weddings?

If your gluteal muscles aren't working properly your hip flexors—the muscles that pull your thighs forward—can become tight, and you can become more prone to injury.

The buttocks are essential for giving you the means to run, move, lift and stabilise your body. They allow you to rise from a seated position, to climb stairs and to stand. Let's just say that your butt plays a very important role in assisting you to get around in life.

So, how does your butt get around? Weird question? Not really.

Are you running around and getting the most out of life? Are you shaking that tail feather? Or are you plopped on the sofa going nowhere? In order to truly get the most out of those butt cheeks … you've got to move! That is precisely what your butt was designed for.

Take a quick look at how you've been travelling through your day. Is your sitting down to moving around ratio in balance?

If not, take your butt for a walk, a squat or a wiggle on the dance floor.

Now, to really connect with your butt and the metaphors you can draw from it, I've composed a few deeper questions that you may want to reflect upon.

Exercise

- Where or what is your cushion in life? Is or are these cushions healthy? Are you perhaps becoming too comfortable? Do you need to start challenging yourself in this area of your life?

- Do you have sufficient padding, or a sufficient safety net in place in your financial life? One that allows you to remain upright during difficult times?

- Do you have the necessary back-up funds to help move you forward with your dreams?

- Do you have sufficient support groups in place to keep you stable during times of high stress?

- Is there sufficient stability in your life to ensure that you are able to make healthy progress—or steps—towards goals that are in alignment with your highest purpose?

☙ Thighs, Hips and Buttocks; Skirts, Pants and Jeans ☙

Once you've taken the necessary time to answer these questions honestly, we can now move on to how we can embellish that bootie!

To enhance the look of the butt, as well as your hips and thighs, it is important to understand the different styles that are available in pants, jeans and skirts, and what works for your leg length, your butt shape and your hip width. Best to do this prior to forking out your hard-earned cash.

SKIRTS, PANTS AND JEANS

When it comes to finding a decent pair of pants, what are the best types to have to ensure that you are able to maximise your closet.

Must-have pants

1. ***Black leggings*** — either jeggings or faux-leather leggings or skinny jeans.

    Essentially, having these types of tighter-fitting pants in your wardrobe allows you to wear a number of your looser tops or sweaters, as well as longer cardis and jackets, while still looking smart.

This style of pant gives your outfit a more modern, edgy and sexy vibe.

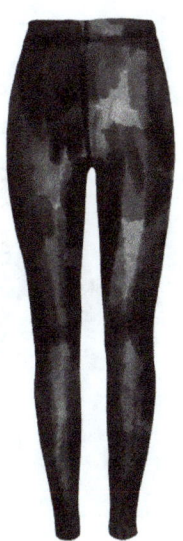

Having something tighter on the bottom half of your body also allows you to balance out the baggy-to-loose ratio, so that you don't appear to be swimming in excess folds of fabric from head to toe. It can also give a sneak peak of how great your tush and legs look, while hiding a larger belly or waistline.

2. **Dark denim jeans** — black or navy — that fit you like a glove.

This allows you to dress your outfit up and down.

If you want smart casual, you can add a dressier top and accessories like a blazer, paired with heels; or you can dress the look down and go as casual as you like with a sweater and flip flops, for example.

☙ Thighs, Hips and Buttocks; Skirts, Pants and Jeans ☙

3. ***Corduroy, khaki <u>or</u> cargo pants***

   These pants often come in sand, beige or olive colours and therefore assist you to maximise your wardrobe. These pant styles also help to add a bit of texture to your outfit. They're also great pants for getting around in when you want to feel comfortable. You might choose to keep the top half of your outfit simple. Perhaps wear a tighter fit if you choose to wear cargo pants, though this is just a suggestion, not a rule.

Corduroy   **Khaki**   **Cargo**

4. ***Dressy pants*** — start with blacks or neutral colours.

   Dressy pants are a style of pant intended as formal or semi-formal wear, and are therefore often made from a higher quality material. They may also come with a matching jacket. Dressy pants can be either a more structured, tailored look—business attire, which can be dressed up for an event—or they can be more feminine and fluid. Another attribute you may find with dressy pants is that the hem length will often sit lower than the ankle line, often covering a stiletto beneath.

5. ***Pants in a bold colour***

Want to add some colour into your wardrobe but a little intimidated by bolder hues? Pop some colour into the lower half of your outfit and even the most conservative amongst us can get away with it. Nothing screams fun, freedom and summer like a pair of boldly coloured capri-style pants. As colour is a key element in design, this is a great way to add interest to an outfit. Also a great base for introducing other colours or prints, or fun accessories.

6. ***Pants with a print/pattern***

These pants allow you to express yourself through a pattern or print rather than through design or form.

7. *Bootleg or flared pants*

This style creates instant length for petite ladies and balances out women with wider shoulders or hips.

I would like to run through different pant, skirt and jean options you can consider, regardless of the length of your legs and the width of your hips and butt. In the measuring up section we will be delving more closely into how to achieve a great fit, but for now, let's just take a brief look at what works for different leg lengths, hip and butt shapes.

Shorter legs (in skirts)

If your legs are on the shorter side, then *mid-length to above-the-knee skirts* are your best ally.

Another way to lengthen shorter legs is to find *skirts that match your skin tone or hosiery*, as this visually elongates the leg.

Adding heels will always resolve the imbalance, particularly if they blend in with the skirt and hosiery colours.

With jeans, a *bootcut style over heels* will add height and a *midrise jean* will give the illusion of longer legs. A darker shade will give the illusion of a thinner, more elongated leg.

Finally, wearing a *lighter colour on the top half of your body*, for example a dark skirt and a light-coloured blouse, will automatically draw a person's attention upwards, towards the top half of your body.

> *It is absolutely essential that what you wear on your torso doesn't go past your hip bone if you want your legs to appear longer.*

Wider hips and butt (but small bust and slimmer shoulders)

Think *darker colours on the lower part of your body*, whether it's a skirt or a pair of pants or jeans.

Thighs, Hips and Buttocks; Skirts, Pants and Jeans

Jeans with curved side seams

Flat-fronted jeans/pants

Flared skirt

For a slimming effect, look for skirts and pants with *vertical designs*, or darts or pleats that draw your attention vertically.

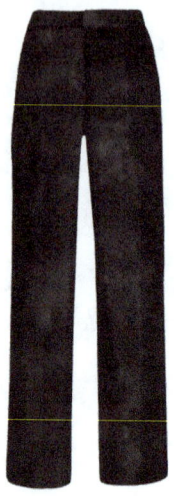 

A *flared style pant* will balance out your hips and de-emphasise the butt. This is the same with skirts. Finding a *skirt that is wider at the base* or is flared will balance your butt and hips. Therefore, *A-line skirts*—these have a fitted waist and gradually flare out to the knee which creates an A shape—as well as *full skirts* will look great on you. You do, however, want to avoid pencil skirts that taper in as they go down, as these will accentuate your wider hip or butt.

If you enjoy the shape of your curvaceous hips and butt, then by all means wear the figure-hugging skirts, these recommendations are only for women wanting to achieve a more balanced figure through their wardrobe options. They are simply guidelines to create balance, not hard and fast rules. There are many very voluptuous women who embrace their curves, and this is when the above guidelines go out the window.

The guidelines go out the window because the other way to deal with your curvaceous body is to be proud of it. If you do this you'll find that it not only turns heads; it shows that you are a confident woman who loves and appreciates who she is, a very sexy quality indeed.

But, for those of you with a little more resistance to your curves, your focus will be to downplay the lower half of your body. This means steering clear of detailed pockets and flaps around the hips and butt area, including embroidery details: essentially anything that will draw attention below your waist.

Instead, direct all of your attention to adding emphasis to the top half of your body, so that your overall silhouette appears more balanced. You can do this by finding blouses and tops that have bows, zippers, sequins, pockets and flaps around the bust or shoulder area.

Top-heavy and flat-bottomed

If, on the other hand, most of your weight is up top (bust), and across the upper section of your body in general (Normally seen with Inverted triangle or V-shaped body types). Then you want to find pants that bring attention downwards. Pants that are either wide legged or boot cut, give more balance to your overall body shape.

Wide Legged Pant

Boot cut style

For jeans—the same rules with pant styles apply to jeans—buy denim with *decorative back pockets and double stitching*. Aside from *boot cut* and *flare* styles, V and H-shaped ladies also look great in tight-fitting skinny jeans as your legs are often your greatest assets. Show them off!

≈ When Glamour Meets Gratitude ≈

Boot cut   Flared   Skinny

Look for a *curved yoke*, such as the v-shaped or sweetheart yoke, as this will give shape to your bottom. Also known as the riser, the yoke is the v-shaped section at the back of jeans. It gives the denim a curved seat, and the deeper the 'v' of the yoke, the greater the curve.

V-shaped Yoke   Sweetheart yoke

Another way to achieve extra shape for your derrière is to look for curved pockets. Curved pockets will make your butt appear perkier too, which also makes your butt look curvier.

≈ Thighs, Hips and Buttocks; Skirts, Pants and Jeans ≈

Flat front pockets or no front pockets remove bulk from the tummy area. Keep any pant detailing to a minimum on the front—where your belly is. The *flatter the front* of the pants (i.e. no flap pockets, embellishments or pleats) the less visible your belly will appear. Keep any detailing and pockets to the hip, thigh and butt area instead.

Flat front pockets   No front pockets

Flap back pockets add bulk to a flatter bottom.

A-line skirts also look good on V and H body shapes. A-line skirts flare out from the waist, creating the illusion of a fuller lower torso whilst sitting flat along the tummy.

A-Line Skirt (above the knee)   A-Line Skirt (longer)

⁌ Thighs, Hips and Buttocks; Skirts, Pants and Jeans ⁍

Wide shoulders and great legs

Wide shoulders, a larger bust, not much of a waist but great legs. If this sounds like you then your body shape is an *inverted triangle*.

Like your H or rectangular sisters, you look great in flare and boot cut pants to help balance out your horizontal body. Cuffed jeans and cargo pants also add visual bulk to your legs, thus helping to balance out the top section.

When it comes to skirts, your figure can wear tiered and tulip skirts as well as peplum skirts. Essentially, any type of skirt that bulks out around the butt and the hips looks good on this figure. Or you can add visual bulk to the hips by wearing skirts with horizontal lines or prints —this works in a similar way to tiered layering.

Tiered skirt   Peplum skirt   Tulip skirt   Ruffled Skirt

Athletic or boyish H-shaped figure

A pleated skirt or flared skirt—especially helpful with a band to cheat a waist—works well for someone with less curves around the waist, hips and bust. These skirts can range from mini to full-length. Also, a skirt with panel detail as well as a full circle skirt work wonders to add bulk to the waist and hip area.

Banded Flared Skirt

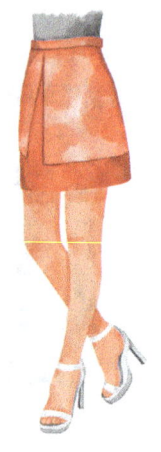

Paneled skirt

Wrap skirt

Long pleated skirt

Short pleated skirt

Jeans styles such as *skinny jeans* are ideal for more rectangular-shaped figures, as legs are often the sexiest asset in a figure that is more athletic. Always remember to highlight what you've got!

Skinny Jeans

Boyfriend jeans are another great jean style for the more athletic body shape. Typically, these are fitted at the hips and in the seat with a more generous, relaxed cut through the leg. Look for boyfriend jeans with strategic rips around the hips and upper thighs, to draw attention to that area.

Boyfriend jeans

Also, *bootcut and flared* jean styles work well. These styles will help to create curves, particularly when combined with a lower-rise waistline.

Bootcut jeans   Flared jeans

In relation to the best pant styles for a more athletic-shaped figure, consider *peg leg harem pants*, as these give the illusion of wider hips and thighs.

Peg leg harem pants

❧ Thighs, Hips and Buttocks; Skirts, Pants and Jeans ☙

Additionally, *flared or wide pants* give the illusion of wider hips and thighs.

Chapter 5

The Reproductive Organs and Underwear Styles

THE REPRODUCTIVE ORGANS

Made up of the vagina, the uterus and the ovaries, these organs serve to express your ultimate feminine creativity by enabling you to give birth.

This is a sacred region for any woman and should be treated as such. The vaginal canal represents the intimacy of the female body and embodies the source of life. Symbolically, this area represents birth—of a child, of new ideas, of intimate connection, creativity and bliss.

Should any of these areas feel a little blah, it is time to look at what is happening at this level.

Has mundane, day-to-day existence robbed you of your passion or creativity? What are the ways you could inject a little more joy into your life? Has your relationship with your mate become a little lacklustre? Is it time to put a little more attention into this area? Do you need a holiday away from the daily stressors to simply reconnect?

Or do you just need to develop a stronger connection with yourself? Do you need to re-explore what gives you bliss?

Whatever you need to do, make sure that you focus as strongly as possible on your feminine energy. The more you find a way of doing things in a fluid, intuitive, receptive and allowing way, the less frustration you will experience.

This means that if any of your creative efforts have been met with hurdle after hurdle, it could be a case of working with too much of your masculine energy, trying to force the issue or 'make things happen'.

Feminine energy is extremely creative; however, it allows things to happen. Feminine energy is patient, it is calm and it knows that there is always a process.

Mother nature knows this too, she simply provides the fertile conditions or the nutrient-rich soil for her seedlings, knowing that sufficient rain and sunlight will permit the seedling to grow into a beautiful plant in its own time.

Sometimes it is important to remember this when all you seem to be faced with is resistance. Just do what you need to from your end, and then enjoy the experience of surrender. Knowing that its seedling will turn into a beautiful plant in its own time and the rest is up to the elements.

Now, from a practical point of view, let's take a look at how to embellish this area of your body.

UNDERWEAR STYLES

Welcome to the joy of underwear!

At times, what you wear under your clothes can have more impact on how you feel than what you are wearing over it.

Why is this?

Because nobody else knows what you are wearing under your clothes, and only those who are truly close to you will be allowed to see what you wear one layer under your dress, skirt or pants.

They're called 'intimates' for a reason, and what you choose to wear beneath your clothes can definitely affect your mood and your confidence.

So, let's take a look at your options now and see which shape or cut of underwear will give you the most comfort and the best line.

Different underwear styles

1. *The bikini*

This underwear style was inspired by bikini bathing suit bottoms and is similar to brief style panties, only with less coverage. The bikini style of underwear gives moderate back coverage and has a waistline—also known as a rise—lower than a brief. It also has leg holes cut a little higher, creating thinner sides than the brief.

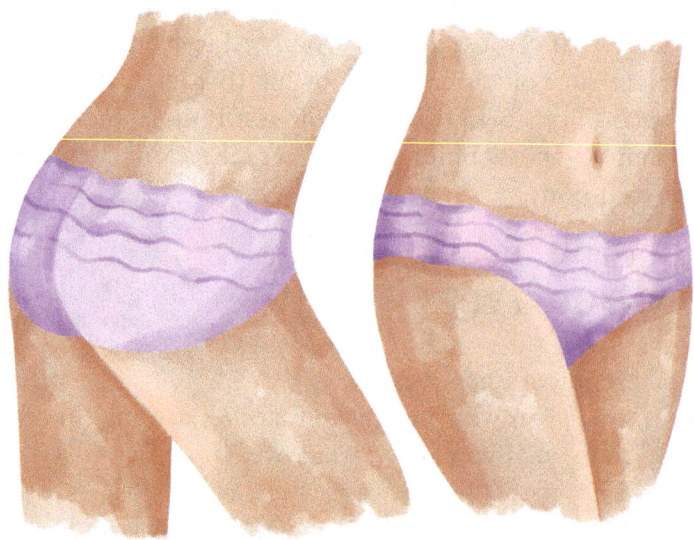

2. *Boy cut or boy shorts*

Named for their similarity to men's boxer briefs, boy shorts have a lower mid-rise waist, provide greater coverage — and modesty — extending to the top of the hips. They are a super comfortable underwear style. They are cut evenly the whole way round and the square-cut leg edge falls below your back cheek, giving them a rectangular shape that is really flattering on most body shapes, and also works to eliminate VPL (visible panty line) under tighter-fitting clothes.

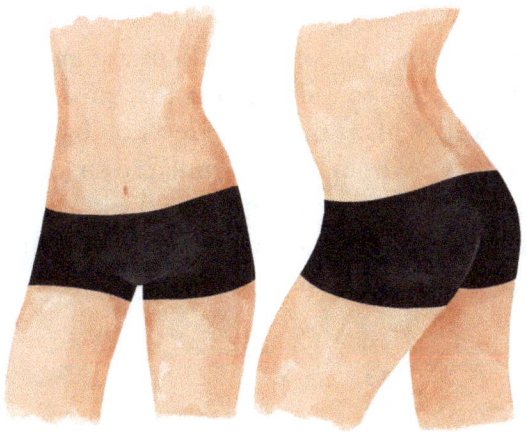

3. Full brief

This brief will definitely give the greatest coverage of all underwear styles. Coverage extends from just below the natural waist—below the navel—all the way to the upper thigh and under your back cheek. Because of this level of coverage this panty style helps to provide a flatter, smoother silhouette.

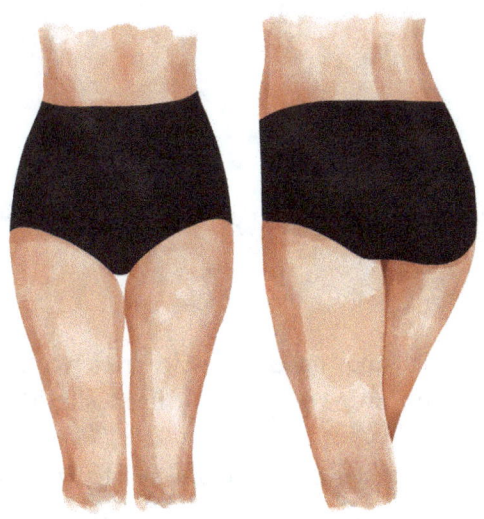

Thong or G-string

The G-String style of panty has a small, often triangular, piece of material covering the front attached to a thin string that runs around the hips and under your back cheek. This is the lowest level of back and side coverage design in underwear. The thong is very similar in shape and coverage; only the thong has a slightly thicker band and a little more coverage on the front and back triangle than the G-string. Both are worn for the purpose of avoiding a panty-line in tight pants, dresses or skirts.

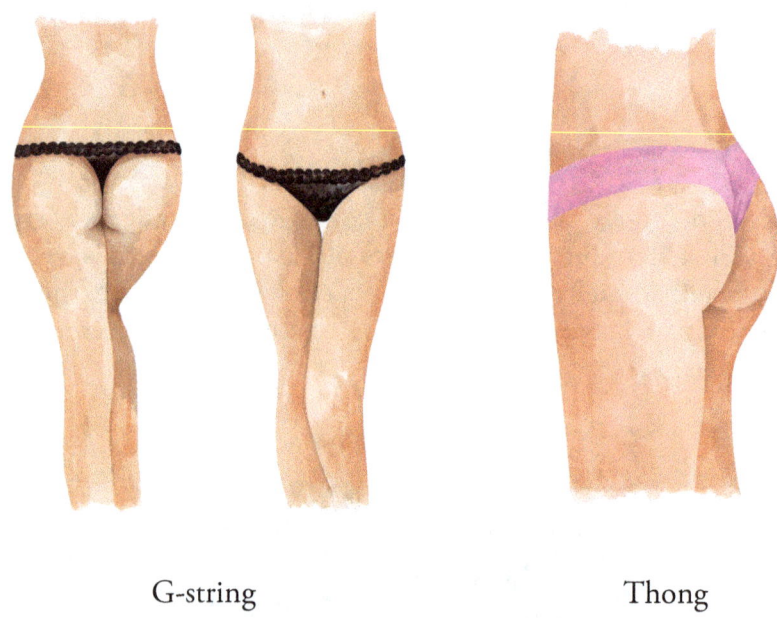

G-string   Thong

Hipster

The hipster is a modern take on the classic brief, with a lower waist-line to hide under mid- and lower-rise pants. It has a slightly wider and higher rise than a bikini.

Hipsters provide great side coverage on the hips without the fabric bulk of boy shorts.

The Reproductive Organs and Underwear Styles

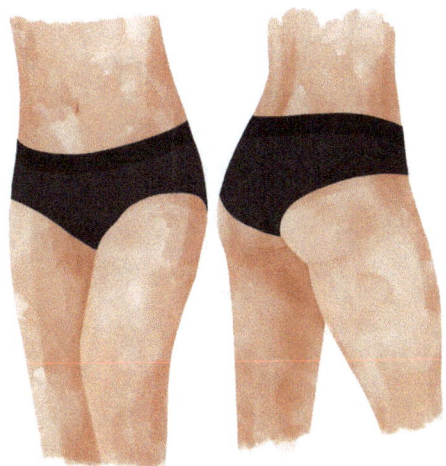

High-cut brief

This style has a higher waist with longer, wider leg openings and thinner side coverage. The higher leg holes make the legs look longer, as more thigh is revealed, while still providing moderate to full coverage.

High-cut briefs with side seams — positioned near the centre front leg — will also provide full back coverage. Without these seams, the back coverage is reduced. They may also provide a certain amount of tummy management, due to the higher rise of this panty style.

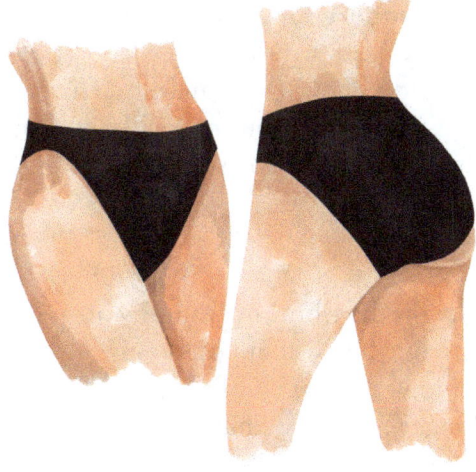

Tanga

This style is mid-way between a bikini and thong. The legs are cut to create a 45-degree angle across the back cheeks. This is more back cheek coverage than a thong yet less than a bikini. They also have wider sides than a thong. A great transition-style underwear if you want to move from briefs to thongs or g-strings.

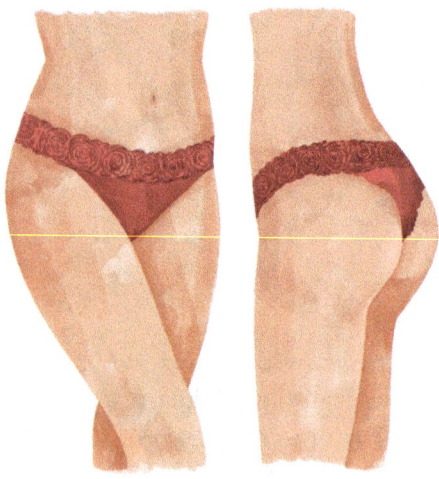

I would like to give credit to Tomima Edmark, founder of HerRoom.com, for her authority on this subject.

Butt shapes and best underwear styles for them

As you no doubt, already know, there are different butt shapes that occur and these are generally linked to your overall body shape. Below is a guide on how to maximize your butt shape through best underwear choices.

Squarer or flatter butt

If you have more weight distribution around your waistline, or if you have a wider pelvis, then your but will appear to just go straight up and down. This makes the butt look squarer and flatter. You'll also find that your torso ends up looking longer as a consequence and that you need to focus on creating curves in this area.

If you're a woman with a squarer or flatter bottom, look for underwear styles with the following features:

- seamless panty styles
- styles that cup the lower back cheek at the creaseline (such as boy shorts)
- you can also wear styles with less back coverage e.g. tangas and thongs

Panty styles that work with your butt

Seamless panty styles — these panties have their seam placed in the centre back of the panty, along with an absence of elastic on the leg edges. This means that no seam-line is visible under clothing.

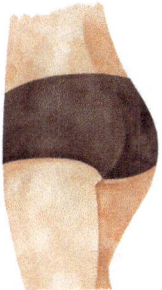

Boycuts and bikini styles — both of these styles are great at showing off the lower curves of the back cheeks and giving the butt a visual lift. Especially flattering are boy shorts that have a scalloped or lacy edge and end in the middle of the back cheeks, as they give a greater illusion of roundness.

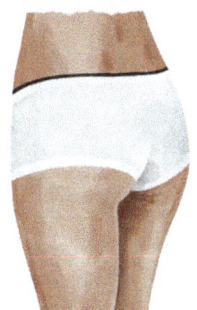 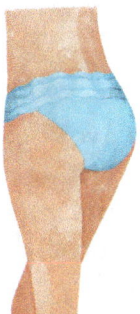

Tangas and thongs —As the focus of these panty styles is towards the centre of the back cheeks as opposed to the edges, the eye ends up seeing everything outside the edges of the back thong or tanga edges as extra padding. As there is a small triangular shape at the top of a thong — and a 45-degree angle at the back of a tanga design — both cut through the often squarer back cheeks of this butt shape, and a visual back cheek roundness is created.

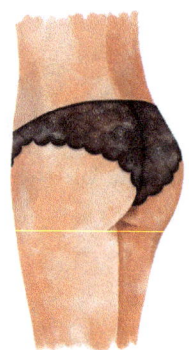
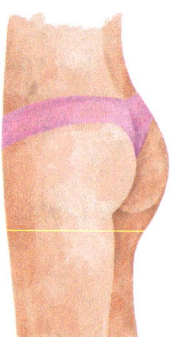

Padded panties — if you wish to create added bulk in this area.

Panty styles to avoid

High cut leg underwear styles — if you want to avoid the 'wedgie effect' of underwear riding up all day, steer clear of this style.

Also avoid any panty styles with fullness around the back leg area, as this will cause gathering or puckering at the back of the panty on a flatter butt.

rarely comes down far enough in the back to give your cheeks coverage.

Round or Bubble-style Bottoms

Here, weight distribution tends to occur on and around the actual back cheeks — the gluteal muscles — and the upper buttocks. This gives this butt shape a fuller, rounder and often a perkier look. This type of butt is widest at the centre of the hips.

If you're a woman with a fuller or rounder bottom, look for underwear styles that include the following features:

- Panties with stretchy material (e.g. lace) or extra fabric to prevent the dreaded wedgie effect that can occur when there isn't enough material.
- Styles that have less back coverage such as tangas, thongs and G-strings
- Panties with a central back seam

Panty styles that work with your butt

Panties with a centre back seam — this panty is ideal for this butt shape as they give the cheeks a better curve and prevent the uni-bottom look that can occur with certain brief and bikini styles.

Boy shorts and tanga styles — create the illusion of a smaller bottom due to cutting across fuller back cheeks.

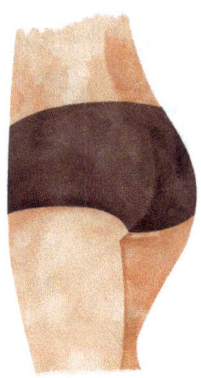

Tanga style — gives you a sexy silhouette without pulling.

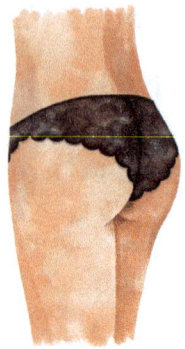

Boy shorts — will give good back coverage and fit because they usually come with a back seam and an inseam.

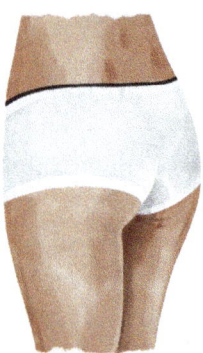

Thong — will fit because there is no back to it.

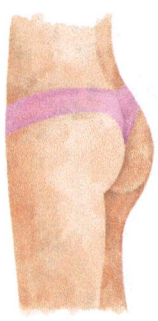

Panty styles to Avoid

High cut leg panties — they will not give enough back coverage and could creep inward.

Non-stretch fabrics — they are too tight across the back cheek section

A-shape (common butt shape with triangular/A shaped women).

This butt shape tends to gain extra volume below the hip bones and is often the result of fuller thighs. This shape is considered one of the most feminine butt shapes due to the tapered effect it gives from the waistline to the hips and base of the butt.

If you're a woman with full thighs and a full bottom, look for underwear styles that have the following features:

- higher-cut styles
- larger leg openings
- no side seams
- laser-cut edges
- made from a stretchier fabric such as lace

Panty styles that work with your butt

Brief and bikini styles with high-cut leg design — this leg-opening style is less restrictive and therefore more comfortable around the thigh.

High cut brief — the higher cut side seam gives a fuller thigh visual length which is somewhat slimming

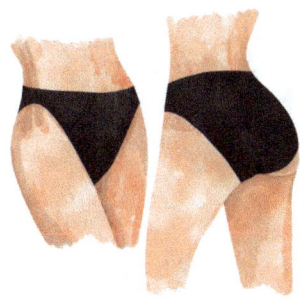

Underwear styles to avoid

Full cut briefs — these will make your butt look bigger.

Underwear styles with smaller leg openings or leg openings with an elasticised edge — they will feel tight around the thighs.

Chapter 6

The Back, Power Posture and Backless Dressing

THE BACK

We are now travelling up to the back. How does it feel? Does it seem tight in areas? What position are you standing or sitting in right now? Are you upright? Hunched? Are you sitting like the letter C? Or do you have posture that would make the mother of etiquette schools, Emily Post, proud?

Constructed from your spinal column, spinal cord and associated nerves, and your vertebra and muscles, your back serves to support you throughout life. Almost like a giant pillar that holds your body upright, keeping its structure in alignment.

The spinal column and brain make up your central nervous system, and my goal here is to help you to understand just how intricate and delicate this system is, and to reveal its magnificence.

Divided into lower, middle and upper sections, the spinal column houses a host of nerves that send messages from the brain to the organs (and back again) via a series of electrical impulses.

As messages are sent from the brain into our bodies via the spinal cord, it makes sense that our body would react in a physical way to our self-talk, our thoughts and our attitudes. It is imperative, therefore, that we start our day by monitoring the self-talk, ideas and attitudes we are allowing our minds to pass into our bodies via this channel.

Exercising Your Support

What supportive and unsupportive messages are you feeding yourself today?

Grab a pen and paper and create two columns. Write at the top of one column 'Supportive Messages' and at the top of the other 'Unsupportive Messages'. Now set a timer for 15 minutes and brainstorm all the thoughts, ideas and worries that have been going through your mind today.

I want you to start with the 'Unsupportive Messages' column, reflecting on the fact that these are messages you have given your body.

- How do these messages make you feel?
- Whereabouts in your body are these feelings located?
- Are these feelings you want to hold onto?

Look at the individual messages.

- Where do you think this message stems from?
- Is this message a reaction to something in the external world, outside of you?
- Who gave you this message?
- Did this message arise in response to something you heard or saw earlier today?
- Is this message a result of comparing yourself to another person?
- Is this message likely to build up or tear down your heartfelt goals and desires?

Now look at the 'Supportive Messages' column, again, reflecting on the fact that these are messages you gave to your body today.

- How do these messages make you feel?
- Whereabouts in your body are these feelings located?
- Do these feelings give you a sense of your own power? Your potential? Do they give you a sense of expansiveness?
- Are you able to tap into one of these messages and hold it for a minute or longer?
- Can you think of ways you can incorporate this type of self-talk and the feelings it generates into your day more often?

Focus on strengthening your body's central supportive column with thoughts of love and gratitude, assisting you to stand firm and upright, in alignment with your highest sense of goodness and self worth.

And speaking of *upright* ... I want you to take a very good look in the mirror and assess your current posture. It's pointless walking around in a glamorous backless dress if you have the posture of a hunchback.

Also, by standing straight you will automatically expand your chest area, which houses your heart. As your heart is the very thing that connects you to everybody else it is important to stand upright, with your chest out. Don't hide your chest; it is an important part of you.

I therefore ask you to stand proud ... chest out! Bum out! Head high!

This body posture brings immediate confidence. Those around you will feel it energetically, and people will respond to your energy in a positive way. More importantly, standing upright will make you feel different within your body, your mind and your heart.

Don't believe me? Then try this exercise ...

Think of something that you would like to explain to someone ... an idea you have. Now roll your shoulders forward, lower your head and stoop your neck. Then imagine looking at another **person and delivering your message from this position.**

Does your message feel as though it will be well **received or** are you feeling a little self-conscious?

As you're explaining your idea, feel into your body. Now, lift your head, straighten your spine, push out your **chest,** lengthen your neck, and deliver your message again. How does that feel? Different?

Your body language and the position — quite literally — from which you speak, has a profound effect on the confidence of your delivery, and therefore the way in which your message is received.

Furthermore, standing tall allows you to breathe better. You are able to take deeper inhalations as well as expire deeper exhalations when your posture is upright. Why does breathing more deeply matter?

Taking the time to breathe gives you the space to think. It controls those knee-jerk reactions that you often regret after the words have already come out. Having more control over your reactions brings a greater sense of calm and creates less drama.

According to research conducted by body language expert Amy Cuddy, you should aim to take up as much space as possible — energetically — before going into a meeting or interview. This state of expansion will make you feel more powerful and, therefore, more confident in the interview.

It was observed that leaders will naturally and physically take up more space in their environment, thereby making their presence felt. Whereas disempowered people will often take up less space and actually try to appear smaller, by hunching over or bringing their limbs inwards.

Power Posture

Obviously, you won't be doing these types of gestures in the meeting or interview. Behind closed doors, however, you can practise any of the following power postures for a couple of minutes prior to an important event or even prior to attending a gathering where you haven't met anyone before and want a quick confidence boost.

Exercises for heightened confidence:

Hands on hips with chest forward and head held high.

The Back, Power Posture and Backless Dressing

Raise your hands above your head.

Lean forward over a table with your hands pressed either side of the bench.

◁ When Glamour Meets Gratitude ▷

Sit at a desk with your hands behind your head and feet placed on the table.

Most importantly ... stand up or sit up straight!

Great posture doesn't only give you a physical benefit, the mind and heart also respond with greater confidence. Confidence helps to create trust and enthusiasm, which is contagious to others. Imagine the improved connections and interactions you'll have, purely by standing up straight.

From here on in, remember that you no longer have to cower and hide yourself. You have every right to take up space on this planet! Standing upright and speaking from a place of alignment will allow others to truly see who you are, and will enable them to engage with you in a more authentic way.

Great exercises that can be done to strengthen the back include yoga and Pilates. However, maintaining good posture on a moment-by-moment basis is of key importance. Now that we understand how important it is to have great posture, we can turn our attention to how to enhance the back through fashion.

BACKLESS DRESSING

Ways to add to the appeal of the back, through the route of fashion.
Nothing screams sensual femininity like a backless dress; however, this is not the easiest outfit to wear. So how do we overcome the obstacle of exposing our backs whilst still offering support to our breasts?

Sew-in-cups

Sew-in-cups are definitely the most secure and comfortable option. This option requires a seamstress, however it's well worth the organisational effort and expense if you want to feel comfortable and secure in your backless dress all night.

Boob tape

Boob tape to secure your breasts in place. Just ensure you cover your nipples with silicone adhesives first, or you could have difficulty removing the tape from this area.

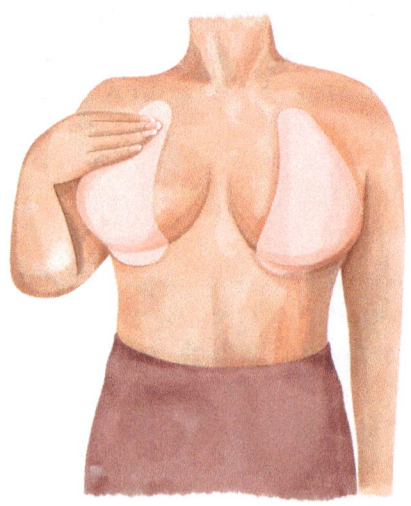

A matching coloured bra

Sometimes it is okay to reveal your bra, if it looks as though it is part of the outfit. However, to pull this look off, the bra you are wearing has to look *hot*! No old, falling-apart bras allowed.

Strapless clear back bra

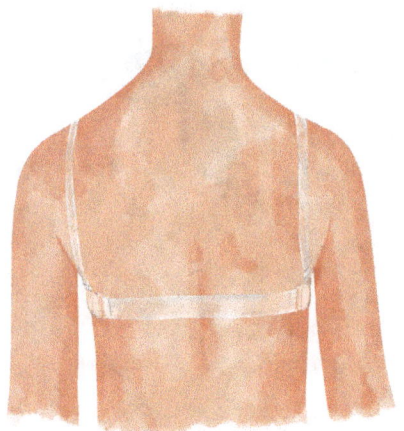

Silicone Nipple Cover

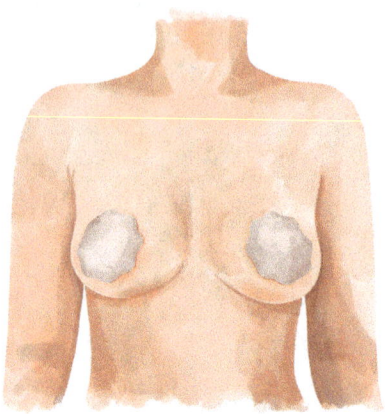

This silicone nipple cover is non-slip and comes off without causing pain.

Wraparound bra with convertible straps

Low back strap attachments are available, and enable you to wear a backless dress with style and sophistication. This bra's straps criss-cross lower than the standard bra straps. They often come with a demi-cup bra style.

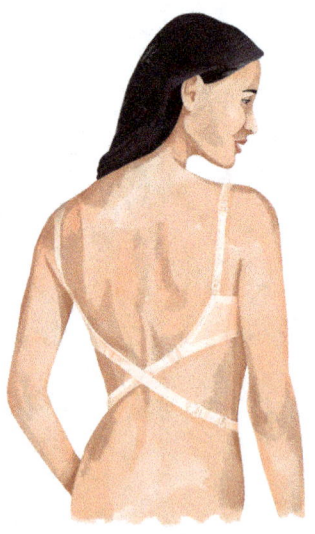

Stick on backless bra

Stick on backless bras are great for smaller- to medium-sized busts.

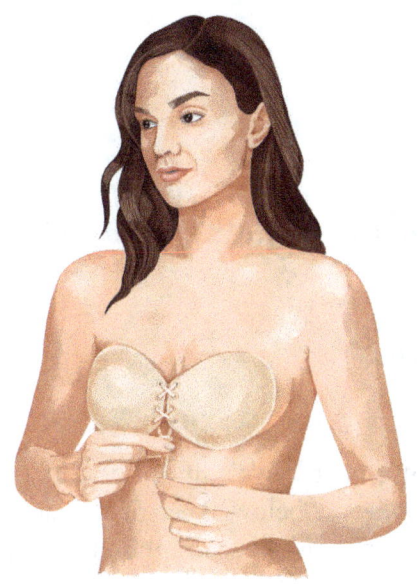

Chapter 7

The Waistline, Your Belly and Dresses

THE WAISTLINE

We're now focusing on the waistline. Look at the area slightly above your belly button and below your ribs. Place both hands on your waist and feel into the muscle of the diaphragm — the uppermost part of the waist.

How much of an indent have you been blessed with here? Do you have a curvy, hourglass figure or are you more of an androgynous, straight up-and-down type in relation to your waist?

There is no need to pass judgement either way — if possible I'd like you to refrain — I just want you to observe. What feelings come up when you look at your waistline? How mobile are you in this area? Are you able to move your waistline with the dexterity of a hula dancer? Or do you require a little more loosening up in this area? Is this something you would consider exploring?

Around the area of the waistband, including slightly above but just under your breasts, we find all of the body's *digestive organs*, such as:

- the *stomach*, which helps store, break down and assimilate food
- the *liver*, which processes useful substances and detoxifies the body from harmful chemicals
- the *gallbladder*, which helps the body break down fatty foods
- the *small intestines*, which assimilate and absorb nutrients from food

- the *pancreas*, which creates fuel for the body from food consumed and regulates blood sugar
- the *spleen*, which is your blood's filtration system

Once all necessary nutrients have been absorbed by these organs, the remaining substances go through a process of filtration and elimination.

A large portion of filtration and elimination takes place in the belly region through the:

- *large intestines (bowels)*
- *kidneys*
- *bladder*

Digestion takes place in the belly region through the digestive organs. To summarise, the digestive organs perform the following crucial roles:

- *take in* life's nutrients
- *process*
- *assimilate*
- *digest* (includes filtration and elimination)
- *feed and regulate* the body
- *keep it performing at optimum health* — provided it is given sufficient nutrition

To facilitate our body's ability to function at its best, we need to carefully *consider what we are taking in* and take the time to consciously digest. This can be symbolically applied to the thoughts, beliefs, ideas, people, situations or circumstances in your life ... in addition to the food you're ingesting. Before your ingest, pause and ask yourself the following questions ...

- Is this healthy?
- Does this benefit my body's ability to function optimally?
- Is this toxic?
- Will this add pressure or burden my system, or throw my body out of balance?

I ask you to do this as frequently as possible, because often we just take in whatever we are given … and we don't bother to question whether or not it is beneficial.

We just automatically consume society's many expectations — in addition to whatever food is in vogue. Suddenly, after a few years of taking in what has been fed to us, we realise we are not taking in what we wanted for ourselves. In fact, we're living society's version of who we should be, what we should do and think and eat. Worst of all … we might not even know who we are or what we want.

The first step is acknowledging that you actually *have power and the ability to decide what you will take in*. Marketing messages, your external environment and other people also have an influence on what you take in … just think of how much extra food you eat when you're in front of the television while hundreds of junk food commercials being broadcast, or even how much extra food you eat with friends and family. Your food intake definitely goes up from what you would normally eat, unless you eat more when you're bored.

However, when you're more present and conscious — this requires a little effort on your part — you will have more time to ask questions and to reflect or analyse whether what you are taking in is actually serving your best interests.

You are not at the mercy of others. You do have the power to exercise choice. There's no need to be subject to a victim mentality. When it comes to what you take in, particularly as a female — because being receptive is part of your natural energy pattern — remember just that you do really have choices and remember to exercise that choice to your advantage.

Choose wisely and you'll experience radiant health. Choose poorly, maintaining negative habits, and you'll experience dis-ease.

Your life is a reflection of all of your mini-habits, all those actions you make on autopilot. *Pay attention to your habits*, in all the areas of your life.

> *When you take the time to chew proper digestion follows.*

If you actually take the time to chew the items that sit on your plate, your body's digestive organs have a much easier job. If we consider this symbolically, if you actually take the time to reflect about the ideas, beliefs and circumstances in your life, you may find that they're not good for you either.

Prior to taking the time to sit and give yourself the time to chew, you may have been taking things into your system without any conscious awareness of what you were absorbing.

When you don't take the time to chew, you generally absorb everything too quickly, in large doses or in an imbalanced way, thinking it will *fill* the gap, the craving, the desire, the hole —whether that hole is in your stomach or in your life.

However, if you are more mindful when you eat and you consciously take the time to chew and assess what you're taking in, and how your body responds to your food choices, a whole new reality emerges. A reality where you're more in control, having greater consciousness and awareness of what works for you and what doesn't.

Remember that word choice? Yes, we *all* have choices. Sometimes they're small and sometimes they're large, but having an awareness that they exist is crucial. Exercise your right to choose in your favour rather than against it. Making choices that are positive and serve you will assist to bring you into your own power.

If you're feeling disempowered, start by taking charge of small choices, such as what you will be eating for dinner tonight. You'll soon find this small, simple act has a knock-on effect in other areas of your life. The way you do the little things in life will begin to automatically translate to the way you do the more important aspects of life, too. *Pay attention to your habits!*

THE BELLY

We're moving down now to the soft region of the belly. How do you feel when you look at this area? What thoughts come to mind? Take out your pen and paper again and write them down. Are your thoughts supportive and praising or are they negative and self deprecating? If it's the latter, would it be possible for you think differently? Could you enjoy rubbing your tummy? Could you like the soft, feminine feel of your belly?

This area of the body houses and protects a number of very essential *organs of elimination*. Considering the incredible role it plays, it is sad that it has become an area of such attack. Often referred to as 'muffin top', and generally considered too flabby, too large, too wide ... the list goes on.

It's true that too much weight in this area can have negative health implications. So it does make sense to keep an eye on your waistline. But self-loathing is not a healthy mindset from which to base your weight loss, if this is something you would like to do.

I realise that not everyone is trying to lose weight, however, to ignore the issue of excess weight in this area and not address the topic would also be quite an oversight on my part. On this topic of excess weight and what to do about it, I would like to suggest the following:

If you're pushing against yourself, in a constant state of inner battle or conflict, or saying 'I hate you' or 'I hate this part of me'; then the energy is of resistance and self-attack. Unfortunately, the more energy you give to something, even if it's about something you don't want in your life, the more power it has. You begin to feel under attack, and respond like a powerless victim. It's all a very negative point from which to start any positive, meaningful endeavour.

Could you turn that mindset around to one of wonder at the amazing function this area performs? Could you ask your belly what it really requires, and why it has felt the need to hold on to its excess weight? Ask it why it chooses the foods that it does? And whether there is a better option for it?

Suddenly you have transformed from a powerless victim to someone who is in control. Someone who knows how amazing this part of their body is, and who wants to listen to it and to assist it to experience greater health. Add a pinch of conscious eating to the equation, where you actually stop to experience the effect the food has on your system after eating it, and you're really heading along a different path.

It's amazing how a shift from self-hate to curiosity and self-love can move mountains. When you don't like something you can't see any of its positives, and it lingers around you like an oppressive cloud. The resistant energy around hatred tends to lead to additional suffering and struggle.

Yet when you love something you want to give it everything it needs to thrive. You move towards what you love with positive energy and intention, and your reward is greater ease in what you're aiming to achieve, as well as personal growth.

I'm not saying that you can't want things to change. Change is a natural part of our being. What I am saying is that when you want something to be different, focus your attention on what you want instead of on what you don't want.

Complaining, criticising, comparing and self-hatred are all examples of focusing on what you don't want. Focusing on what you do want would be more along the lines of, 'Okay, I'm currently this weight or dress size, and I would like to move towards this weight or that dress size."

You can then ask yourself questions such as *What are people who are my desired dress size or weight doing differently to what I am doing?* Then you can start incorporating these different habits or behaviours into your day.

If you've never exercised, going straight into boot camp mode is going to be very difficult. If you haven't dieted, putting yourself on a strict diet will be equally tough. Instead of something that's hard to achieve, just add *one* healthy step into your day. Ultimately, whether it's diet or exercise, your final aim is to become healthy, not to lose weight. The weight loss will happen automatically and stay off when you do become healthy.

You could choose to go for a daily walk or swim, for example. Something that you know you can stick to, because it's not too onerous. The discipline of this action will feel good after a while. Once, and only once this has become a standard part of your day, you could consider upping the pace and going for a jog each day instead of your walk. Then, once jogging becomes a natural habit, you might then feel a desire to start boot camp.

While all this is happening, you might feel an inclination to eat more fruits and vegetables. You may naturally start associating with other people who are trying to achieve greater health, leading to different conversations and influences. It will start happening instinctively.

You might choose to replace your fizzy drinks with water. Water is essential in helping your body to eliminate waste, thereby increasing your metabolism, and it's common knowledge that better metabolism leads to increased weight loss.

You may also start by having one serving of veggies, then you want to know how to cook another vegetable. You research it and it tastes better than you expected. And before you know it, you're making healthier, more nutrient-rich food choices. As you give your body what it needs, it will reward you with enhanced vitality. Exercising and eating a healthier diet will begin to feel natural and good.

When you finally look down, you'll see that your belly and waistline have shrunk, despite not having forced yourself into it. You haven't put yourself down; you haven't called yourself fat and ugly. You've just created healthier habits that you've executed consistently, and the *results of your choices have naturally been reflected.*

Now you're in a different headspace, reflecting your new activities and thoughts. You simply decided to make different and more empowering *choices*. In the process of making new choices, and acting upon them, you BECAME a healthier person.

I've used bold for the word BECAME, because this is what matters most. Not the end result: the weight loss. It was who you *became* in the process of slimming down. You BECAME healthier. When you become healthier you maintain your figure. Eating healthily and exercising are consistent habits of a healthy person. When you become a healthy person you will maintain healthy habits; therefore, you will manifest a trim figure.

Weight loss *on its own* is not healthy. Many diets require drastic and unbalanced ways of eating, and are not sustainable. You may become skinnier temporarily, but it won't last because to maintain weight loss you need a sustainable way of eating, and this equates to a healthy way of eating. And it is who you become through being healthy that matters, not the quick fix.

We all have the power of choice. Exercise that power from a position of self-love and awe at how incredible your body is. It's simply about making that choice.

So regardless of how you feel about your belly region, I want you to take a moment to reflect on what this area of your body does for you. The belly region houses and protects organs such as the bladder, which is connected to the kidneys; and the large intestine, enabling the body to filter, eliminate and release all of the processed waste that doesn't serve your body. This section of the body is keeping you alive; it's your personal sewerage system.

Holding on to toxins is not a way that anyone should live their life. Unfortunately, however, many people do live their lives this way —holding on to experiences, ideas, people, belief systems and circumstances that no longer serve them.

Inner release exercise

Think of old patterns and belief systems that you may be holding on to that no longer serve you; there are probably many that you have unconsciously inherited from family, friends and society. Do you really believe them? Do they assist you in the life you want to lead? Find your pen and paper to make notes.

The Waistline, Your Belly and Dresses

A great way of symbolically helping with this exercise is to have a large glass of water next to you, as you focus on this region.

- Can you think of any non-helpful thoughts and beliefs, or previous circumstances, that you already know you need to let go?
- Is there someone you need to forgive?
- Are there past circumstances you still feel guilty about?
- Are there any situations — such as a job, a relationship or a friendship — that don't serve you anymore? Something you've held onto just because it's familiar? Something you've learned to tolerate?
- What are the things, people or circumstances in your life that give you a feeling of heaviness? Could you drop or let go of them?

I'm not saying you need to go out tomorrow and de-friend everyone on Facebook, quit your job and erase an entire group of people from your life. However, I would urge you to start releasing the negative emotions you hold around these people or situations.

Concentrate on one of the negative thoughts, heavy feelings or situations. What emotions do you feel? In a similar way to assessing a part of your body objectively or dispassionately, I am now asking you to do the same with your emotions. Allow them to be, and just sit with them: as if you're sharing a room with the emotion and are engaged in an eye-gazing exercise. Imagine that you're in one chair and the feelings are sitting in another. *Do not run away!* Be present. Remember the times you've resisted your emotions or tried to fix them and it hasn't worked. So try something new — just feel. Give any emotion that arises your undivided attention. For as long and as much as it needs. Just be with it and accept it and love it, then release it out of your life.

If you're doing this exercise properly you will start to feel your body release many unwanted emotions. You may need to carve out a bit of time to really process the emotions. As much as possible, maintain your focus on your body's sensations during this process. Your body speaks volumes and is often, if not always, a better barometer of what's good and bad for you than your mind is. The mind just speaks louder. You only discover the power of your body's knowledge when you are able to turn down the mind's chatter volume and tune into your body's channel.

Once you feel calmer within your body, pick up your glass of water. Hold the glass in your hands and think of someone or some experience that you really love. Focus on the feeling of love and gratitude. Now imagine sending that loving energy into the water you're about to drink. Believe me …this is a much more effective detox method than any crash diet.

Speaking of a mental detox … today, as you look at your belly in the mirror, I ask that instead of the usual criticism it regularly receives, send it thoughts of gratitude and appreciation for the incredible role it performs.

For not only does it house and protect the organs of elimination and filtration, *it also houses nature's greatest creative powerhouse — the uterus and the ovaries.*

Your ovaries are in charge of starting the reproductive process and your uterus has the capacity to house a growing foetus. Life begins its process right here, behind your belly button; it's your connection to your life force.

If you really want to benefit from the energy that sits in the belly — the deep reservoir of creativity housed here — take a moment to breath into this area prior to undertaking any creative process. Whether it is painting, crafting, singing, writing, playing a musical instrument, cooking or gardening. Whatever it is you're about to create: just breathe into your belly first and watch what unfolds.

So, yes, we all need to keep an eye on our waistlines for health reasons, but it is imperative that we learn to love this area of our body for the amazing role it plays in our lives. Please show gratitude and appreciation to your belly, regardless of its size.

Remember, each body shape is different and tends to gather weight in a different region. For example, one body type might store weight around the shoulders, another may gain weight on the hips and buttocks, whereas some tend to gain weight around the belly, waist and bustline first.

If your body gains weight around the mid-section or belly first, then I understand your frustration. A tank top just isn't an item of clothing in your wardrobe unless, of course, you've managed to *really* embrace this region … in which case … I commend you!

DRESSES

Showing off your waistline!

A great way to show off your gorgeous waistline is to display it in a beautiful, feminine dress. The type of dress line that is best suited to your body type can be found below.

To understand what will suit your shape best, you need to look in the mirror and see whether you have a waist that is slim and accentuated relative to your hips and shoulders. Alternatively, you may have a waist that is relatively wide in relation to your hips and shoulders. There is no right or wrong shape. You just need to recognize your shape and work with it. This is when you'll look your best. Trying to make your figure something that it is not will only make you look and feel uncomfortable and ill-fitting.

Are you curvy or are you more straight up-and-down? Understanding how different dress styles enhance different physiques will definitely give you an edge when it comes to getting all dolled up. Below you'll find some of the most common dress styles, as well as details about which silhouettes they flatter the most.

Dress Styles

Basque or dropped V-Waist dress

This style of dress has a V-shaped, or U shaped, section at or just below the waist. It's almost like a corset, as it has a closely contoured fit to the top section. This dress style works to accentuate the hips, and it suits curvy, short-waisted and wide-hipped figures.

Bias Cut dress

This dress actually refers to the orientation of the fabric, rather than the cut of the dress itself. The threads in the fabric run diagonally, instead of horizontally, allowing the fabric to drape gracefully over the curves of the body whilst ensuring that the hemline is smooth and straight. This leads to the fabric appearing softer, thinner and more fluid or stretchy than dresses that are cut horizontally or vertically.

It looks particularly impressive on an hourglass figure, due to their curvaceous body types. Even if you don't have an hourglass figure, if your body type (somatotype) is fuller and more curvaceous, this is a brilliant cut for any woman with curves due to the fluidity and movement of this dress style.

Empire waist dress

The empire-waist dress falls above the natural waistline, creating a false waistline just below the bust. This is great for women with short torsos or wider waistlines. This style of dress also helps to disguise a larger tummy, or enhance your bustline.

Princess cut dress

This style has a fitted bodice that tapers at the waist, then falls freely. This helps create the illusion of a slimmer figure, without hugging the tummy. It's a great option for women who are a little self-conscious of their tummy or hips.

Halter dress

The halter dress defines both the bust and shoulders, and is secured at the back of the neck and waistline. It's often a casual or summer dress, but can be made more formal with the use of certain fabrics and embellishments. This style is great for most body types, but is especially flattering on women with broader shoulders relative to their hips. The dress's neckline creates a diagonal line across the shoulders, reducing the broadness of the shoulder area.

Wrap dress

This dress wraps around the body. In doing so it enhances the bust, by lifting and separating; reduces the waist, creating the illusion of an hourglass silhouette; and reduces the hip, by drawing the attention upwards towards the bust. This is a very versatile style of dress, as it accentuates a curvy physique beautifully. As this style of dress lends to more fluid fabric that drapes and moves with the body it is especially complimentary to fuller silhouettes. For women with a more angular body (less curves) look for stiffer fabrics and more structured versions of this dress.

≈ The Waistline, Your Belly and Dresses ≈

Tunic

Another versatile style, as it can be dressed up or made more casual. They generally sit at about knee length, and can be worn belted or unbelted, and with or without tights. Can be worn by any body type. Shift dresses without a belt look great on women with less waist definition.

For women with waist definition a belt will make this dress look and feel less boxy on your form.

Style Tips to Help Visually Reduce a Larger Waistline and Belly

When a protruding tummy or lack of waist are affecting your style confidence, you may find yourself believing that your only fashion options are a sack. Not true. Below are a handful of styling tricks that will help to deflect attention away from your waist, allowing you to stop focusing on these problem areas and start focusing on your assets instead!

Find tops and tunics that skim your waist and belly region, rather than cling. Tops that drape or ruche are also preferable. For this reason, you don't want to tuck tops into pants or skirts, as doing so will only make you appear wider.

The Waistline, Your Belly and Dresses

Use vertical stripes as a pattern or create vertical lines with your clothing, through the use of long cardigans, jackets, vests or ponchos. The aim of creating vertical lines is to elongate the figure, rather than enhancing the figure's roundness. In this way, you are helping to disguise your belly. Remember, however, that the skinnier the stripe the more slimming it will be.

Blouses and dresses with darts — princess seams — create the illusion of a waist when they run under the breast (see the image on the left). They slim the entire top section when they run under the breast all the way to the waist. If you work in an office environment, look out for these types of outfits, as they are suitable for office wear, as well as being slimming.

◈ THE WAISTLINE, YOUR BELLY AND DRESSES ◈

Choose pants and skirts that are free of detail across the belly. Ensure pants and skirts sit flat on the belly. Look for pants and skirts with openings or zips at the side rather than at the front of the garment, wherever possible.

Prints with diagonal lines pointing in at different angles will create a slimming effect across the midline. Also, tops with asymmetric hemlines work to cut through the belly area in a similar way to a diagonal print line.

◆ WHEN GLAMOUR MEETS GRATITUDE ◆

Darker coloured clothing (this doesn't mean you have to wear black all the time, just a darker column of colour) will make you appear slimmer.

As you can see below, our eye is automatically drawn to the break in colour on the body of the lady on the left. Our brain turns her figure into two separate parts. An upper and lower half. In this case we notice the break between the base of her top and the tops of her trousers, which is what occurs when you have contrasting tones (light and dark).

However, if you don't want any attention drawn to your midline because you have a waist that is wider than your bust for example, a column of colour will cause the viewer's eyes to run up your silhouette without any need to pause anywhere which in turn makes you appear slimmer and taller.

Visually cut up your waistline by layering tops, cardigans or jackets over pants, so they end at different lengths.

⌇ The Waistline, Your Belly and Dresses ⌇

Wear clothes that fit! I've already mentioned looking for tops that drape and don't cling to the waist and tummy area. If you wear clothes that are too tight in this region, you will feel uncomfortable and the clothing won't sit smoothly. On the other hand, wearing a top that is too large will make you look wider than you really are. Well-fitting clothes look better on everyone.

Chapter 8

Bust, Bras, the Breath and Necklines

BUST

The next area we're observing is the chest and diaphragm. When you look in the mirror you see your breasts, as well as the skin covering your rib cage.

Pay attention to this area.

- Are you happy with what you see?
- How much padding do you have?
- Are your breasts proportionate to the rest of your body?
- Or are they larger or smaller?

Maybe you feel your boobs are too big, too saggy, too small, or that your nipples are the wrong colour. We're all very good at finding fault, but I implore you to look in the mirror and give thanks *regardless* of what you perceive to be 'imperfectly' formed breasts.

The breasts provide nourishment to newborns, and they serve as a cushion to comfort others when we hold them close and nurture them. Nature's cushions … imagine that!

BRAS

When such a wide selection of tops and necklines is available, it goes without saying that different bras will be the best option for different outfits. So, I'll be providing a breakdown of the different bra types. First things first, though. If you want your bra to do its job correctly and shape your form while giving you maximum support, you need to ensure that you're selecting a bra that fits you properly.

In order for your bra to be both comfortable and supportive, there are two areas that need to fit properly:

- Firstly, the fit across your breasts and the way they sit in their cups
- Secondly, how the rest of the bra fits your body, particularly across your back and over your shoulders

To properly understand what makes a bra fit well; it is easiest to begin by identifying the features of a poorly fitting bra.

What are the indicators of an ill-fitting bra?

- Your straps are loose and keep falling down
- Your straps need regular adjusting (tightening) or are digging into your shoulders
- The band at the back of the bra rides up your back
- The sides of the bra cut into the sides of your bust, creating underarm and/or back bulging
- The gore isn't sitting flat against your chest: it's lifting; meaning you need a larger cup size
- On the other hand, if the bra-cup size is too big, there will be excess material in the cup, causing it to wrinkle rather than sitting flat against the chest

Understanding the composition of your bra

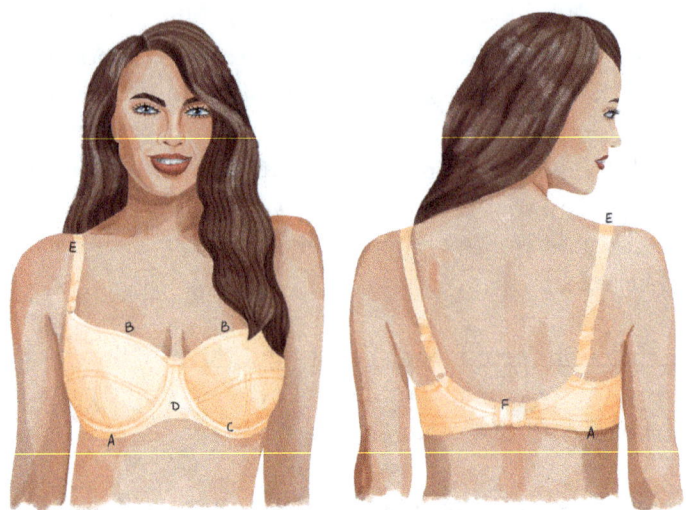

A - Band; B - Cups ; C - Underwire; D - Gore; E - Side panels; F - Closures.

The bra is composed of several main parts. Understanding what they are and why they're part of the bra's construction will assist in helping you find a bra that fits correctly.

Band

Ninety per cent of your bra's support comes from this section of the bra. The band of the bra runs around your rib cage, starting at your underbust area and continuing around your rib cage to your back. The band holds the majority of the weight of your bust, meaning this measurement *must be right* in order to have a comfortable and supportive bra.

Knowing your underbust measurement — when leaning forward, lying on your back and standing — will help you to obtain a perfectly fitting bra. The band is also the central element of the bra, meaning most of the other sections of the bra either connect to it or are part of it.

You will obtain your band measurement from your underbust area — without wearing a bra. You'll know that your band is too big if it doesn't sit parallel on your back. If it rides up, this means your band size is too big. If it cuts in, this means your band size is too small.

Bra cups

The cups of your bra are the pieces of foam covering material (although sometimes a bra is constructed from material with no foam) that hold your breast in place. The cups are sewn into the front of your bra band. There will generally be a front strap attached — or that can attach, unless it is a strapless bra — to the top of the bra cup. Sizes range from A-cup all the way to H-cup. Above this size you'll need to have a custom bra made. However, bra cup sizes only exist in relation to band widths, meaning there are no universal bra cup sizes.

The breasts should sit comfortably in their cups. This means the gore and the underwire (see image above), as well as the cups; sit snuggly against the chest. If the bra cup size is too big, there will be excess material that will wrinkle, and the cups themselves won't sit securely against the breast. You can determine your bra cup measurement by measuring around your torso to the front of your bust peak. Take this measurement whilst not wearing a bra.

If you look at this website: https://www.abrathatfits.org/calculator.php you will be asked for different measurements, which you can type into the designated boxes. Once you have entered in your details, in either centimetres or inches, it will determine your bra size according to sizing specifications in the UK, Europe, USA, Australia/NZ and Japan. Whoever created this resource needs to be applauded!

Underwire

The underwire is a metallic- or plastic-shaped insert that is sewn into the bra cup itself. It is generally a U-shape, however it also comes in a C-shape. It extends from the gore to the armpit section of the bra, and should encompass all the breast tissue that sits in the bra cup, as well as providing an extra level of support and lift to the bust.

The C-shaped underwire is generally found in push-up bras. Unlike the U-shaped underwire, which pushes the bust upwards, the C-shape tends to push the bust closer together, giving more of a cleavage effect.

Gore

The gore of the bra is the central panel that holds the two cups together and is part of the band itself. The gore should sit flush against your chest or sternum. A good test is to raise both arms in the air. If the gore still sits flush against your torso, that's great. If the gore lifts, it means that your cups are not deep enough and you therefore need to go up a cup size.

If your gore is significantly pulling away from your chest then you probably need to go up several cup sizes as well as another band size.

Side panels

These help to support and push the sides of the breast tissue forward and into the cup.

Closures

Hook and eye closures are located on the band itself. They usually sit at the centre of the back, and generally have several hook closures to enable the band to be brought in or out according to loss of elasticity in the bra band, or due to weight gain or loss.

Front closures use plastic clasps at the centre of the front of the chest.

When trying on bands for fit it is best to try it on the last (or widest) hook setting. A good fit on the last hook of the bra will assist you to gain maximum longevity from your bra. Over time, as your bra is worn and washed on a regular basis, it begins to lose elasticity. Being able narrow the width of the bra band means you will be able to wear it for longer.

Straps

These are an integral part of your bra that sit over the shoulders. They help to adjust the height of your bra cup by way of bra sliders, and then keep the cups in place. In an ideal world your bust peak should sit exactly at the central point between your shoulder and your elbow crease. Straps should always sit securely on the shoulders and not dig in. If you need to keep tightening your bra straps, this means that your band is too loose, and you should go down a band size.

Apex

The apex is the part of the bra that joins the straps to the cup.

Ring

The ring is the plastic or metal non-moveable join, through which the straps connect to the band of the bra.

Sliders

The sliders are the clips that sit on the bra straps, enabling you to loosen or tighten your bra strap and therefore lower or raise the height of your bra cup.

Strap join

At the front of the bra, the strap join lies between the strap and the cup. At the back, the strap join lies between the back of the strap and the band. The type of join you see on the back strap is actually quite important. There is a curved joining section that has strap material sewn into the band and connects to the band with a ring. This ring is then connected to the strap. The fact that the band is incorporated into this join, called the leotard join, provides better weight distribution of the breast throughout the band, meaning it is more supportive and less taxing on the shoulder line.

Now that you know the anatomy of a well-fitting bra and how to enable a correct fit, it is time to discover the best bra styles for your bust.

Different bra styles and their benefits

Balcony or Balconette Bra

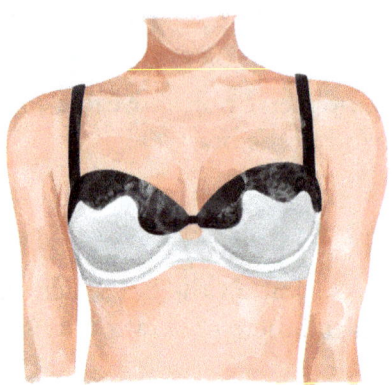

The balcony or balconette bra is typically a half- or three-quarter coverage bra that lifts the top half of your breasts. It provides a dramatic lift to the bust as well as creating a sexy, rounded cleavage. This is a great bra for women wearing low-cut or wide necklines styles, such as V-neck, scoop, square neck or sweetheart.

Plunge Bra

The plunge bra is a popular special occasion, low-cut bra that can be worn under plunging necklines. A plunge bra is perfect for deep V-neckline or other very low-cut neckline tops and dresses, as the angled cups and narrow centre gore create the appearance of increased cleavage.

Padded Bras

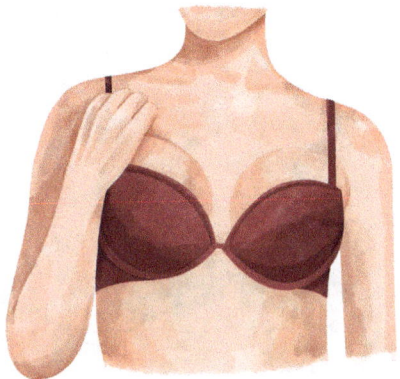

Padded bras have strategically placed padding at the bottom of the bra to make the breast appear larger at the base. This bra style pushes the bust up and sometimes inwards as well — if the underwire comes in a C-shape rather than a U-shape. This causes the upper bust to be more fully revealed, leading to a larger-looking bust.

T-Shirt bra

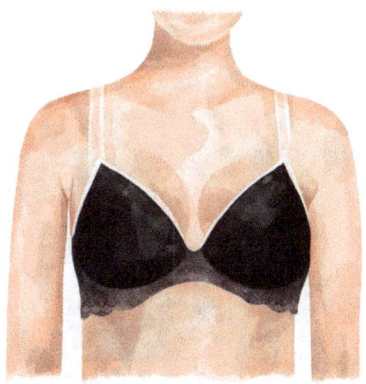

The T-shirt bra has thinly cut padding designed to be invisible under tighter tops. This bra style has smoothly moulded cups for added support, and provides a rounder breast shape under clothing.

Full cup bras

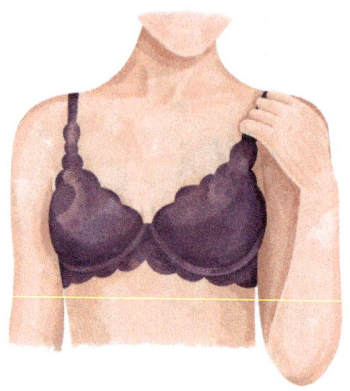

Full cup bras offer women with larger and fuller breasts a sense of comfort, support and coverage. This bra style completely covers the breast, while also lifting the bust up and forward, providing maximum comfort. The lift helps to create a division between the waistline and the bust, which can sometimes get lost when a fuller bust projects over the natural waist.

Sports Bras

Sports bras come in different styles, however their main function is to help reduce breast movement while exercising. If the bust size is smaller, a compression style sports bra will help to contain bust bounce. It works in a similar way to having a bandage strapped around the bust.

If the bust is fuller, a full-cup style sports bra that covers the entire breast, known as an encapsulation-style sports bra is a more comfortable option. Notice features such as a high central panel (gore), wider straps, full coverage of the breast and additional fabric at the top of the cups. These features work together to securely encapsulate the bust and reduce bust movement during strenuous workouts.

Demi Bra/Multi-way Bra

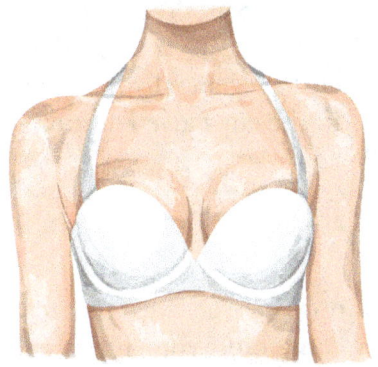

A demi-bra, often also used as a multi-way bra, is a half-cup bra. It gives a corset effect to the bust, meaning the top of the bust is more prominent, as well as making the bust appear fuller. It also creates extra cleavage and lift — as well as structure — to its wearer. This style bra looks amazing and invisible under low-cut and wide neckline garments. However, due to the decreased coverage in the cups, most of the support in this bra comes from the band. In addition, the straps are often placed at wider points on the band, enabling the bra to be used as a multi-way bra, including halter-neck, backless and strapless styles.

Minimiser bra style

The minimizer bra helps to flatten out your bust through compression. Alternately, they push the bust up and then redistribute breast tissue evenly throughout the cup with the use of a wider-based underwire than the standard U-shape. The straps are generally quite wide, helping to keep bust in place. Also, the seams in the cups give additional support to the bust.

THE BREATH

Let's go a little deeper now, to the area protected by breast tissue: it's safeguarding the region containing your lungs and your heart. Not only do you have fatty projections — your breasts — protecting the heart and lungs, but the rib cage doubles up to create an extra level of armour from the outside world. It's incredible to realise just how clever the body is in protecting it true treasures.

Sheltered beneath the lungs, and therefore very closely connected, is the heart. The heart, with all its arteries, produces a life-giving palpitation, which regulates the flow of blood, or the life force, throughout the body. Remember, however, that the heart acts as a two-way pump: sending out oxygenated blood and then receiving and recycling what is sent back via the veins — through the venous system.

The symbolism here is very clear. In order for your heart to truly function effectively, you must learn to both give and receive love.

You *must* love yourself in order to fully love others. There is simply no other way to truly experience and express love. It's a cycle, a rhythm; a perfect balance of give and take. Pull yourself out of balance emotionally and your body will feel this energetically, and fall out of balance physically.

Looking now at what the chest area houses and protects, I want to start by looking at the lungs. The function of the lungs is to fully and freely take in life-giving oxygen. They work in conjunction with the nose and sinus cavities to filter the air that we breathe.

If we look at the yogic philosophy and principles, we find that breathing is one of the core concepts of yoga. You don't have much control over your digestive system, your circulatory, hormonal or nervous system. You do, however, have a certain amount of control over your respiratory system, as you can control your breath to a certain degree. Focused breathing also has a knock-on effect for the body's other systems. Taking three deep breaths can quiet the mind and the nervous system; the knock on effect is better digestion, more conscious mental responses, and greater calm in general.

Obviously, yoga involves a lot more than just breathing, and has a complex number of *asanas* — yoga postures — specifically designed to work on improving specific channels, called *nadis*, of energy pathways through the body, assisting the body's well-being. The very act of breathing is what gives life, as oxygen is required to keep the mind and body working.

It appears that the simple process of knowing how to breathe properly has been lost in today's hectic world. Instead of breathing deeply, many people spend the day holding their breath, anticipating the worst, or are in a constant state of stress and dis-ease.

Instead of simply breathing deeply when tired or out of whack, our modern culture reaches for a coffee to perk them up and keep them going. Alternately, they crash out on the couch and flick on the television. Or they smoke or drink to relax and switch off.

Taking the time to breathe in deeply will cost you nothing, but it will bring you a sense of calm, clarity, presence and focus almost immediately. Apparently, we're only allocated a certain number of breaths in our lifetime, so why not experience each of those allocated breaths more fully?

Keep in mind that each deep breath reinforces your aliveness. This moment, right now, is all you have. So please take the time to acknowledge its beauty. The more you take the time to breathe, the more you'll find yourself in the present moment, in a state of love, and when this happens the whole chest area expands, giving you an increased ability to take in life.

So, next time you look in the mirror and see a chest and rib cage that you either like or dislike; remember the incredible purpose this region of your body serves, and consider how you could be improving its effectiveness. It could simply be a case of receiving and giving more love; it could be about assessing whether or not what you are taking in is actually serving you well.

Let's move on to how you can enhance and celebrate the chest area visually through fashion, by paying attention to the neckline of the tops, blouses and dresses you choose to wear. Choosing the right neckline is like selecting the best frame for an artwork, only the artwork in this case is your face. In addition, as you will see, wearing the correct neckline also helps balance out the proportions of your body, creating a more harmonious silhouette.

NECKLINES

Suitable necklines for women with a smaller bust

When it comes to necklines for women with a smaller bust, the aim is to create more bulk or detail in the décolletage and neck area, and to keep the lines *higher*, generally speaking, though there are times when rules should be broken. Also, wearing necklines that help to widen the shoulder line will create the illusion of a bigger bust.

Speaking of high necklines, you really can't get higher than the turtleneck. Combine a turtleneck with either a deep V-shaped necklace or a rounder and chunkier statement necklace, over the top of the bust, and you'll be creating a harmonious, well-balanced look.

Turtleneck (High Neckline)

By wearing this style of neckline — one that effectively hugs the neck and contours to the true lines of the body underneath — you're creating an elegant aesthetic. This style of neckline works particularly well on a smaller bust because it draws the attention above the chest and adds visual bulk at the collar-line area.

Crew Neckline

The crew neckline style is very popular for T-shirts and sweaters. The height of this neckline, which sits at the collar line area, creates the illusion of larger bust and helps to cut the length of the facial structure.

This neckline looks good with a collar necklace that mimics the crew neckline shape, or with a bib-style necklace.

Boat neck / Bateau line / Sabrina neckline

This neckline draws attention above the chest and along the collarbone, thereby creating visual width along the shoulder line. This is also a great style for women with a longer neck, narrower shoulders in relation to their hips, a narrower face or smaller bust, as it helps to balance out these features.

◁ When Glamour Meets Gratitude ▷

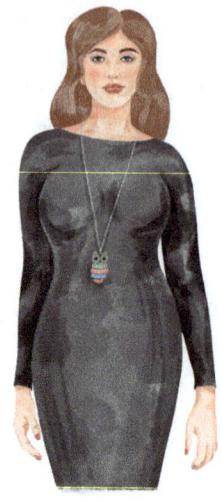

The best necklace styles for this neckline are longer strands of beads or a low-hanging pendant.

Plunge V-Neck

There is the possibility that you will have moments in your life, such as a hot date night, where you want to turn heads and reveal a little bit more than just your collarbones. Well, it just so happens that you are one of the lucky few that can get away with one of the most revealing necklines available and still look classy in the process.

Those with a modest chest can pull this off ... while still looking sexy and sophisticated. This daring style will ensure that all attention is on you, whilst achieving an elongating effect on your silhouette at the same time.

This style of neckline suits a choker style necklace to balance it out. Another option is a longer V-shaped pendant that has layered strands.

Cowl Neckline

The cowl neckline works well for both large- and small-busted women. In relation to women with a smaller bust, the cowl adds shape and volume, through fabric, to the chest area; helping to balance it out. Look for cowl necklines that have thicker folds or material, and fall around the bust area.

This neckline suits a choker, but only if you have a thinner, longer neck. Otherwise, it is fine to leave this neckline free of necklaces and focus your attention on dangly earrings or large hoops instead.

Sweetheart Neckline

This is a versatile neckline that can be worn by women with larger and smaller breasts.

The reason it works well for small busts is because the curves of the v-neckline variation work to create the illusion of curves across the chest.

This neckline has enough shape to not require a necklace. However, if you do want to wear a necklace with a sweetheart neckline, rounded or v-shaped necklace styles work best.

If you are aiming to create a sense of width along the decolletage, however, no necklace works better to achieve this, as it will encourage the eye to continue looking outwards, towards your shoulders.

Suitable Necklines for women with larger bust:

When it comes to a larger bust, the aim is to reduce the width of the chest area by looking for necklines that are deeper. What these necklines do is visually elongate the neck and décolletage area, thereby reducing the roundness of the bust.

V-Neckline

This is the ideal neckline for women with a shorter neck, wider jawline and broader shoulders, as it elongates the face and draws attention to the center of their bodies, and therefore away from their outer edges, thereby achieving a slimming effect. The V-shape cuts through the roundness of the chest area instead of accentuating it, as a higher, rounder neckline might do.

This neckline suits a longer set of beads that hang in an elongated U-shape past the lowest point of the V of the neckline, or a V-shaped pendant that mimics the V-neckline.

Scoop Neckline

A round neckline, commonly found on many tops, sweaters, dresses; and even some jackets.

A bustier woman, or a woman with wider shoulders would look for a narrower scoop, as it brings the attention to the centre of the body, similar in effect to the V-neckline.

The scoop neckline can be worn on almost every silhouette, because it's an open style that helps to elongate a neck that is shorter or thicker, whilst displaying the collarbone area.

The scoop neckline on a larger bust looks great with either chunkier beads, or multiple strands of beads mimicking the scoop.

Sweetheart Neckline

The sweetheart neckline acts as a shapelier version of the V-neckline, and therefore can be worn on most silhouettes.

It's great for women with a larger bust and curves, as it helps to accentuate cleavage. The shape of this neckline also helps to visually elongate the face, and is therefore great for women with a short chin and neck.

The sweetheart neckline can be worn without a necklace, due to already having an interesting shape. Alternately, a rounder, chunkier statement necklace would also suit this neckline, while nicely filling in the décolletage area.

Square Neckline

The square neckline does a great job of balancing out a rounder face shape and drawing attention to the collarbone and décolletage area. This is a particularly sensual part of a woman, so a neckline that enhances this area is a definite winner.

The neckline cuts straight down and across the bust, which is a great thing if you want to de-emphasise the size of your bust or cleavage. At the same time it works to elongate your upper body, which is what you want when you have a fuller bust, as it gives a slimming effect.

A square neckline worn in conjunction with a rounder necklace creates a harmonious balance in the décolletage area. An angular pendant also suits this neckline.

Cowl Neckline

The cowl is a versatile neckline. It creates the illusion of a larger bust for those with less in this area, yet is ideal for women with larger busts as it draws attention towards the face and, dependent on the cowl style, will generally draw attention downwards towards the centre of the chest. This has a minimising effect on the bust and gives a leaner appearance to the wearer. If this is what you're intending, ensure you look for cowl necklines with thinner drape widths, and make sure the neckline sits lower on the body.

Chapter 9

Shoulders, Stress and Sleeves

SHOULDERS

Moving outwards now, to the shoulders, arms and hands. I want you to really pay attention to your shoulders, your arms and your hands. Start at your shoulder line. Look at yourself in the mirror and examine the evenness of your shoulder line.

- Is one shoulder sitting higher than the other?
- Are your shoulders rolled forward?
- Are they tight, sitting up around your neck?
- Is the skin smooth or rough?
- Is there redness or skin irritation?
- Or is it smooth and glowing?
- What feelings are you experiencing in your shoulders?
- Are they feeling tight or tender?
- Are they feeling hot or cold; is there a tingling sensation anywhere in this area?

Just make a mental note of what is going on for you in this area. No judgement is permitted at this time. Just observe.

Our shoulders are capable of bearing a great load. They are the most mobile joints in the body, enabling the arms to lift up and down, towards and away from the body, to rotate inwards and outwards: you can also flex and extend the arms.

Your shoulders help you to lift and carry and bear weight: from oversized handbags to small children, in addition to the emotional pressure of everyone in your circle of friends and family.

My question, however, is how much of a load do you really need to carry?

Whether at work, emotionally, or at home; if your shoulders are up around your ears rather than comfortable, relaxed and permitting your necks its full range of movement, I invite you to start creating a plan for how you can lighten your load.

It appears that women have lost sight of the sensual nature of their shoulders because they're taking on daily financial and family stresses instead. Women in Western cultures tend to suffer on their own, as they often don't have the support of extended family members to help raise children, an option that is generally much more available in non-Western cultures.

The price of independence can be overwhelming, however, and the stress of such a constant and ongoing high level of solo responsibility can take its toll.

Do you really need to take life's burdens on ALL BY YOURSELF? There is, after all, a world out there to support you if you just let others know how you're feeling.

However, sometimes it's a little difficult to express how you are feeling when you can't even admit how you are feeling… to yourself.

As someone who would always declare "Anyway!", whenever a difficult or uneasy feeling about a situation arose, I came to realize that feelings have to be acknowledged, and fully felt, for the heart to be able to properly integrate them.

Brushing them aside with the "Anyway!" statement, required me to constantly keep busy doing or even thinking about how to solve problems. "Anyway" didn't give any room for feelings.

Below is a simple exercise to get you out of your head, back into your body …and ultimately into your heart.

De-stress Exercise

1. Sit down, close your eyes and take a deep breath in and out (repeat several times)
2. On your next inhale bring your shoulders up towards your ears

Shoulders, Stress and Sleeves

3. On your next exhale release your shoulders down (repeat steps 2 & 3 several times)
4. Become aware of any of the sensations in your body -hot/cold, pain, tingling or vibration, numbness etc
5. Keep your attention running up and down the body feeling into these bodily sensations a little deeper for a few more breaths
6. And now just become aware of anything that comes to mind. It might be something that's been happening at work, with your children, partner or friends. It could be something you're struggling with. It could be a memory that has surfaced. Whatever it is, don't try to force it. The mind never really stops so just allow whatever wants to show up for you to do just that.
7. Now that you have a situation in front of you, don't try to problem solve it. Instead, just feel into your body. Notice how your body feels about this situation. Really explore the response your body has to this situation through bodily sensations. It could be pulsation, numbness, tingling, heat/cold. Whatever it is, just notice it in response to what you are holding in your mind.
8. Once you've done this for a few breaths turn your attention to the emotions you are currently feeling around this situation. It might surprise you just how much of an emotional response you have to this situation. Don't judge the emotions that arise. Just be aware of them. This is always the first step to healing. Give this to yourself!
9. To close your meditation practice bring something that you are grateful for to mind. Something or someone you love. Really feel the emotion of gratitude and let it run right through your body.
10. Feel into the souls of your feet and the palms of your hands, notice your seat against your chair and slowly begin to open your eyes.

It's from this space that you can reach out to others. It's a much more connected space. A heart-based state. You'll find that allowing yourself to receive help and connection in general from others is precisely what your heart most often needs.

It can be hard to recognise the power that resides in your shoulders when you're exhausted. What you will feel is how much tension they can hold, in addition to the weight they are carrying. This is not a glamorous look, nor is it a glamorous feeling.

If you take a moment to look at your shoulders in their relaxed state, you'll notice that they possess a very seductive, sensual and appealing pride of place. Having already read the section on necklines, I'm sure that you're aware that the correct top can enhance and flatter their appearance.

To you they may just be your shoulders; revealed the correct way, however, shoulders really can cause quite the stir. They offer a little sneak peak, indicating there is more to be revealed, only … you're *only* revealing your shoulders … *Suitors, will you just calm down already!*

Shoulders really are an alluring female calling card, when they're displayed in a relaxed state. Therefore it is essential to understand the basic guidelines of how to enhance them, depending on your shoulder line.

Not everyone has shoulders they wish to expose. Also, it's not always appropriate to bare your shoulders. Having an understanding of the type of sleeve that best shows off your shoulder line, however, is a great place to start.

Revealing your shoulders according to your body type

In their design, sleeves should complement the bodice of the garment; functionally, sleeves should provide ease of movement, as well as comfort; ideally, in the arena of fashion, your shoulders should also provide a point of balance for your hips.

From a fashion or design perspective, this means that if your shoulders fall into the category of 'too broad' or 'too narrow' — in proportion to your hips — it may be difficult to find clothing that sits comfortably on your shoulders without being too loose or tight in the rest of the garment.

If you have either of these shoulder issues, read on, because I'm going to focus on how to overcome this hurdle when it comes to selecting sleeves that best flatter shoulders that naturally sit wider or narrower than your hip line.

Let's begin with our broad-shouldered beauties …

SLEEVES

Best sleeves for women with Broad Shoulders

Raglan sleeves

The seam of a standard shirtsleeve runs from the armpit over the shoulder; however, the raglan sleeve runs diagonally, under the armpit, up to the collar. This diagonal line will help break up the square look of the shoulder, as well as drawing the eye downwards to the armpit, instead of towards the shoulder. This way, you are cutting diagonally through the shoulder line, reducing the visual width, and this assists by softening any sharp edges in your silhouette.

The raglan sleeve is also more comfortable than most, as it permits the arms to move more freely. That's why this style is regularly used in sports clothing.

Another benefit of this style is its capacity to use different colours as a feature of the style. A dark colour at the shoulder is particularly beneficial for creating a receding effect at the shoulder line.

Dolman Sleeves

Dolman sleeves have wide armholes that taper to a tight wrist, or end in a diagonal. This sleeve style is often cut in one piece with the bodice, so that if you extend your arms out sideways it looks like you have batwings. This style leads to a straighter line from the armpit to the waistline, meaning the broadness of the shoulder line is less obvious. This style of sleeve works well with tighter fitting pants, such as skinny jeans.

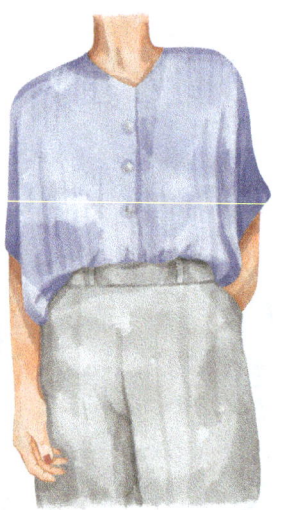

Butterfly sleeves

Butterfly sleeves are a loose fitting, flowing style of sleeve, with a wide base and gathered lines. It's ideal for women with larger arms and shoulders, as any bulky lines are lost in folds of the sleeve itself.

≈ SHOULDERS, STRESS AND SLEEVES ≈

Kimono Sleeves

Drawn from traditional Japanese dress, the kimono sleeve has been adapted to Western fashion. These are wide, loose sleeves — either short or wrist length — cut as one piece with the bodice. Due to this factor, there are no shoulder or armhole seams, meaning the garment falls directly from the shoulders. This draws attention away from the shoulders, as the eye naturally travels downwards to the widest section of the sleeve, away from the shoulder line. Just remember that the endpoint of the sleeve is where the eye will stop. If you are wide in the waist then you don't want to add extra bulk to your waistline by having a sleeve finishing at the elbow. If this is an issue for you, look for sleeves that end lower down the arm.

When Glamour Meets Gratitude

※ SHOULDERS, STRESS AND SLEEVES ※

Bell Sleeves

Bell sleeves are narrow at shoulders and gradually widen as they reach the wrist, which they do especially below the elbow. This design works to balance broader shoulders.

Different styles can be created in this sleeve by cutting any length from the upper arm, the elbow, the lower arm or the wrist. Remember this when choosing your garment because it will add visual bulk wherever the flare is at its greatest.

Or any sleeve with lot of detail near the shoulder

The logic behind the sleeves to avoid is that you do not want to create an additional impression of width on your shoulders. Width lower down on the sleeve is welcome.

Best sleeves for women with Narrow Shoulders

We're now moving to our narrow-shouldered sisters. The downside of narrow shoulders is the continual readjustment of anything that sits on your shoulder line, for example bra straps, or sleeves that sit on the shoulder edges.

The upside narrow shoulders, however, is that you really have the opportunity to play with all the elements of fashion in this area of your body. This includes being able to wear bare shouldered styles, as well as adding zippers, buttons, bows or epaulettes to the shoulder line, as these will all widen the appearance of your shoulders.

As far as sleeves go, extra fabric and shoulder detail is your best friend.

Shoulder pads

Natural, skin-coloured, rounded shoulder pads are the best option.

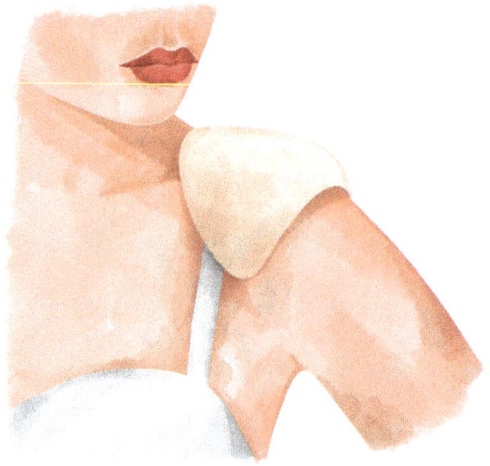

Puff sleeves

Add volume to your shoulders by looking for styles that gather or puff at the shoulders. This additional volume will make your shoulders appear larger, or at least more closely proportional to your hips.

Juliet sleeves (Also known as 'Leg of Mutton' sleeves)

This style of sleeve is little less puffy than a puffed sleeve and is also generally longer. It's great for women with narrow shoulders and slender arms.

Horizontal epaulettes or embellishments

Look for sleeves with horizontal epaulettes or embellishments at the shoulders, such as lace, beading, ruffles or zippers. By adding bulk to this area, you are visually widening the shoulder line.

Set-in sleeves

Set-in sleeves are created by a shoulder seam that fits directly beneath the shoulders. This makes the sleeve curve, creating an illusion of wider shoulders.

Cap sleeves *(specifically shorter cap sleeves)*

A shorter cap sleeve sits over the shoulder line (like a cap) but doesn't extend along the underside of the arm; instead, it tapers away to nothing at the underarm. This gives a visual impression of widening the shoulder line and is, therefore, a great sleeve option for enhancing narrow shoulders.

Avoid *dropped shoulder sleeves*, as this style draws more attention to the narrowness of your shoulders.

Chapter 10

Arms and Hands – and Wrist Enhancements

ARMS AND HANDS

Moving down now to the arms. Look at these lovely limbs that dangle from your shoulder sockets. They're amazing: they swing, lift, bend, reach, grab. These long appendages allow you to take on and carry so much in life. Even if you feel as though your arms are too flabby, too long, too short, too hairy, too skinny — or you happen to be blessed with beautiful, slender, perfect-length arms — what really matters is how you use them.

These limbs are constantly in motion: collecting items you need, assisting you in your work and reaching out to all you hold dear. You can't hug someone without your arms. Think of all of the intimacy you would miss out on without arms. They are a natural extension of your heart and lungs, and allow you to reach out to others as well as joining them in a mutual embrace.

Our arms are joined to our wrists and hands, and this allows us to touch, grasp and let go of objects. They are used as tools for greeting and friendship. Our hands also help us to express ourselves more fully. Take away your native language and watch your hands go to work in an attempt to convey your emotions and thoughts to somebody who speaks a different language from yours. Whether you find yourself drawing pictures with your hands to explain yourself or make charade-type gestures, it's your hands that will be there when language fails.

Hands are amazingly creative. They can express our creativity through painting, cooking, sculpting, building, sewing, knitting, playing a musical instrument or writing. We only need to look at the etymology of the word, derived from the Latin word *manus* (meaning hand) to see how closely our hands are linked to our identity.

The hands can show tenderness through a loving caress, or anger through a slap or a punch. The handshake originated as a way of confirming that neither you nor the person you were greeting was carrying any weapon. It's easy to see, therefore, why trust between individuals is often represented through the shaking of hands, as well as its use as a polite greeting.

Many healers use their hands to massage, manipulate or send therapeutic energies to the recipient. Hands are also our primary sense organs — they assist us to discover heat and coldness, hardness and softness, as well as texture, pressure and vibrations. Fingertips are highly sensitive, enabling a high level of perception that helps us respond to our environment.

However, you choose to use them, make sure your hands are extensions of love and kindness, and they will serve you well.

HONOURING YOUR HANDS AND ARMS

> *Create your own very easy cuticle oil*

There is nothing more irritating than hangnails. During the winter months, these tiny bits of excess skin around the cuticles can become extremely painful, especially if you begin tearing at them. Not only are they painful, however, they can make the hands appear rather unsightly. Therefore, if you know yourself (and know that you just can't stop pulling at these excess bits of skin), the most effective form of attack is prevention.

Having a bottle of cuticle oil next to your bed that makes it easy to apply to your cuticles each night is the ideal solution.

You could even consider soaking your cuticles in oil now. Grab a small bowl and add a few drops of any of the following oils:

- carrot oil
- jojoba oil
- avocado oil
- olive oil

- coconut oil (which you could melt in a bain-marie or place a teaspoon in the microwave for 10 seconds until it loosely melts).

The above oils are known as carrier oils, and they provide a base for your essential oils.

Now it is just a matter of adding a drop of essential oil — such as lavender, rose, rosemary, lemon, or your favourite blend — into your carrier oil and then massage this into your cuticles. You can also push your cuticles back with a cuticle stick for a more manicured effect. Do this regularly. Minimum, on a weekly basis and your hands will *love* you for it.

> Simple hand and arm moisturiser recipe

Making a body moisturiser can be as easy or complex as you want it to be. For the purpose of this exercise I want to keep things super simple, to make it easy for you take action.

You can follow a similar method to the cuticle oil in the creation of your hand and arm moisturiser. In order to create a moisturiser of any kind, you need a carrier (or base) of some description. When it comes to hands and arms, you want a deeply nourishing effect, so you would use richer or thicker oils that become solid at room temperature — these are known as butters. An example of these types of oils are:

- unrefined coconut oil
- shea butter
- hemp seed butter
- mango butter
- kokum butter

You can purchase these butters/oils quite readily online. It's a good idea to test different oils and butters at a store first, however, to see which type of texture you most prefer on your skin.

Once you have your butter, melt a small quantity (1-2tbsp) on a stove top, or place it in the microwave for 10 seconds. Once it's melted, add essential oils of choice to the blend. What scent would you like to choose?

It could be a pre-mixed blend of oils that you select or simply a single scent. One or two drops is sufficient, unless you are making a larger batch.

Stir your mix together, leave it to set in the fridge for an hour or so, and then you're ready to apply it!

This recipe is for immediate use and would need to be used within a week. There are many additional ingredients you could use, such a beeswax, to help firm up your cream, so it's not necessary to store it in the fridge to keep it solid. You can also play around with a blend of other oils to reduce the thick texture of the moisturiser.

You could even add ingredients such as glycerine and preservatives, but that's another book or blogpost. I want this to be a simple exercise that is quick and easy, and involves using what is on hand for the purpose of self-care. Even the act of making your own hand and arm cream is a mini gift to yourself. Following this with the act of massaging the beautifully scented creation into your skin is a display of self-love that your body will appreciate. It will also respond by providing you with smoother, moister skin!

To continue the expression of gratitude and appreciation for your hands and arms, it is now time to delve into all the ways to physically embellish and display your hands and arms to the world.

This is the area of the body where your accessories love to hang out. Look at your current accessories. Do you like the watch, bracelet, rings, purse or handbag that you see there? If not, perhaps it's time for an upgrade.

What special treat could you buy for those pretty wrists and hands?

BRACELETS — AND OTHER WRIST-ENHANCING ACCESSORIES

The use of any accessory is a great way to add your personality to your wardrobe. You could have the most basic, neutral — well-fitting, of course — outfit on, and by simply adding a bag, ring, bracelet, scarf, pair of shoes, hat etc. you've drawn people's interest.

It's like having a blank room with white walls and a cream sofa as your starting point. The simple addition of an eye-catching rug, a beautiful painting, bright and colourful cushions, plants and a vase of flowers can completely transform the room.

I'm inviting you to think this way about your accessories. Select each of them very consciously. You want to ensure that they really resonate with who you are — whether that's dainty, bold, funky or classic.

Look down at your wrists and hands. Ask yourself whether you prefer golds or silvers, single or multiple strands of beads, or multiple thin bangles? Do you like the jingle-jangle sound of bangles on your wrists as you move them? Do you like gemstones? Precious or semi-precious? Do you like the look and feel of leather, wood, feathers or tassels? Do you like rhinestones and studs? Do you like broader and larger-scale accessories that are simple and contemporary in style? Or do you like intricate detail?

How carefully manicured are your nails? Are they tidy and polished? Do you like a lot of colour or interesting designs on your nails? Do you prefer nudes? Or do you like to keep this area free of any embellishment?

Believe it or not each one of these factors adds up, helping you to select the perfect wrist enhancements for your hands.

Bracelets can actually be used very strategically. They can distract the eye away from the bust and shoulders, for example, and make you focus more on the hips and thighs, as this is where a wrist enhancement will sit. The daintier and smaller scale the wrist enhancement, the less impact it will have on the overall silhouette, though it can still work to tie the outfit together. However, the larger, brighter and more layered the wrist enhancement, the more it will affect how a person's eye will travel around your silhouette.

Bracelets come in a wide range of colours, sizes, styles and materials, and are a great way of updating an outfit and keeping your wardrobe on trend. Different wrist enhancements suit different social situations, too, and will have a strong impact on how casual or formal an outfit appears to the viewer. Ultimately, wrist enhancements go along with other accessories, to pull your outfit together by completing its final touches.

It is imperative, therefore, that your hands and nails are always kept neat and tidy — if you wish to gain maximum impact from your wrist enhancements, that is. You don't want to grab peoples' attention with your stunning bracelet, only to show off chipped nail polish or unkempt nails.

Wearing wrist enhancements will draw attention to your hands and nails, so I invite you to take a look at the different types available, in order that you decide what would best suit your sense of style and your personal preference.

Types of Bracelets

Bangles

Bangles are a non-adjustable form of bracelet, due to their design. They are constructed in a solid, single piece, and are designed to slide over the wrist. Originating in India, bangles signify good fortune and prosperity to the wearer, and play an important role in Indian wedding ceremonies.

Bangles come in a variety of materials, from gold or silver with encrusted gemstones, to plastic, wood, glass or less-precious metals, and allow the wearer to build them by layering (in the case of finer bangles) or to wear them individually. Layering (also known as stacking) finer bangles is a great way for women with more delicate proportions to generate impact in this area.

Beaded Bracelet

A beaded bracelet is a little more flexible, both in design and function. Beaded bracelets are often brightly coloured, making them a little more fun for styling. They can transform casual outfits and come in elastic or clasp form. Beaded bracelets are an excellent addition if you like the Boho style of dressing.

☙ When Glamour Meets Gratitude ❧

Wrist Cuffs

A wrist cuff is a single, solid bracelet. It's larger in scale than most bangles or bracelets and, therefore, creates more of a statement piece, that can be worn on its own. Wrist cuffs come in a variety of materials and thicknesses, metals and leathers. They are a little more flexible than bangles, and it's easier to adjust them to fit the wrist more precisely. This is due to their design (oval or wrist-shaped), meaning they can be pulled apart and resized reasonably easily. This also means they don't travel up and down your wrists as much as bangles. They are generally secured with snaps, clasps or buttons to hold them in place.

Charm Bracelets

Charm bracelets are a form of bracelet with small, individual charms or symbols attached to a chain. Both the charms and the bracelets are made from a variety of materials — from cheap plastic to gold or silver embedded with precious gems. The value of the bracelet will be determined by the materials used. Charms are sold individually and are a great way to commemorate special events, celebrate milestones, protect the wearer to ward off evil spirits, express religious beliefs, or simply to enjoy the personal significance of each symbol. The fact that you can change each charm according to mood or occasion makes these bracelets extremely popular, as well as a good special and personalised gift option, due to the symbolism they carry.

Elastic/stretch bracelets

Elastic or stretch bracelets are highly versatile and are available in multiple colours, bead designs and widths. They are easy to wear and apply to the wrist, due to their design, which slides over the wrist and then remains fixed in place due to the nature of elastic. These types of bracelets are often cheap to purchase, and can be a fun and simple DIY craft project for those wanting to experiment with jewellery making.

Link (or chain) bracelets

Link (or chain) bracelets are a simple, classic, flexible metal bracelet, comprised of a serious of links. These links are similar to a chain, though generally larger in size. This style of bracelet can be a simple silver or gold chain style, or can be more ornate, such as each link being jewel encrusted, or of a different shape to a standard chain link. This style of bracelet is easy to match to most outfits.

Tennis Bracelets

A tennis bracelet is the term used for a more ornate, precious, gem-encrusted version of the link bracelet. A tennis bracelet is also more delicate in design than a link bracelet.

Wrist watch

There is nothing more timeless and classic, delicate, or contemporary than a wrist watch. An elegant watch can last for decades, whereas more funky and fashionable designs allow you to chop and change your outfit, and can create a statement on its own. Watch bands come in leather, plastic, elastic fabric or are created with links for greater comfort. Watch faces now come in a variety of shapes, to better suit the wearer. Practical yet classy or fun-loving, a wrist watch that reflects your personality and sense of style will keep you punctual and aware of the importance of respecting your own and other people's time.

When Glamour Meets Gratitude

Top tips for successfully accessorising your outfit with a bracelet

> *Keep your colours in the same tone.*

Golds are warmer tones and silvers are cooler tones. There are no longer any hard and fast rules around only wearing gold or silver separately. Especially since dual toned jewellery came into fashion. However, if you want to accentuate warm skin tones- gold, copper or bronze would look best. Also, if you want to accentuate cooler skin tones then silver or platinum would be best. (More detail on colour tones and palettes can be found in Chapter 18.) There are many colours to choose from: the main deciding factor for successful accessory use is whether you look better in gold or silver. Once you know this, you're in a better position to select alternate colours to better enhance your skin tone.

Give your wrist some space by wearing appropriate sleeve lengths — ones that enable you to show off your wrist enhancements. If you don't have enough exposed wrist your bracelet doesn't have the space to be fully appreciated. Wrist cuffs and stacked bracelets or bangles look best with three-quarter or shorter sleeve lengths.

Keep stacking to one wrist. If you layer your bracelets (some thin and others thick is a great blend) in order to make a statement, it's better to do so on one wrist, as this enables you to create a focal point with impact.

Ensure your wrist enhancements match your unique scale. This will be discussed in detail in Chapter 17. For the time being, however, keep in mind that it is important to select wrist accessories that match your proportions. If you have small wrists and hands, wearing a large bracelet will overwhelm your wrist. If you want to add more drama to your wrist use multiple strands or layers of finer bangles/bracelets. If your wrists and hands are large, by contrast, then delicate wrist enhancements have minimal impact, so choose a larger or bolder style.

Don't like to wear much on your wrists? A manicure will ensure your hands are noticed for the right reasons, and will show the world that you take care of yourself. The definition of 'manicure' is to have something trimmed or neatly maintained. At the very least, keep your hands and nails neat and tidy. Even if it's just a case of keeping a file and cuticle oil or cream beside your bed at night and applying it before sleep, your hands will reward you for this service.

GIVING AND RECEIVING — A NIGHT-TIME ROUTINE

Perhaps you could make it an evening ritual to reflect on how you used your hands at the end of each day? A reflective practice is great to have at the end of each evening. Below are some questions you might wish to reflect on before bed.

Journal on the following questions — once you've applied your cuticle cream, of course!

- Who and how did you greet someone today?
- Did you create anything new or heartfelt?
- Who or what did you pick up, grasp or push away?
- Were you able to give freely? Or were you holding back? If so, why (or why not)?
- What and how were you willing to receive today?
- Are you clinging too tightly to anything?
- Is there something you need to let go of or that you fear letting go of?
- Who do you need to reach out to?
- Who do you need to hug or hold close?

Once you've taken the time to reflect, place your hands together in the prayer position, press them over your heart — in between your breasts — close your eyes and breathe deeply for a few minutes. Think of people you love and how grateful you are for them. Hold that feeling of gratitude for several minutes, then send this feeling from your heart, down through your arms and into your hands. With this feeling of calm appreciation you will be able to better create, connect, reach out to and express who you really are through your hands and arms when you awake.

Chapter 11
Neck and Throat: Scarves and Scarf Styles

THE NECK

I invite you to take a closer look at your neck. The neck gives us a range of movement, sideways as well as up and down (the nod) and in a semi-circular fashion (looking around—scoping out the joint). If you drive, then you will know that your car follows the direction of your neck. It is actually your neck that steers your car. If your car is symbolic of the way your life is travelling at the present moment — and your neck is steering that direction — then what is your neck telling you?

In the movie *My Big Fat Greek Wedding* the mother turns to her daughter and says, 'Your father may be the head of the family, but the woman is the neck that turns the head.' This mother realised just how powerful she was, in addition to understanding the influence the neck plays in directing affairs. The reason the neck is so powerful in its influence is because it sits in between the head and the heart, the two energetic centres of the body. (The mind and heart have their own electrical impulses and circuitry.)

The neck, therefore, plays a central role in connecting your head to your heart, while taking in your immediate surrounding environment. When you are in front of the computer or are studying for extended periods of time, is it any wonder that you have strained, cramped neck muscles? Your neck is trying to tell you, 'Okay, information overload! I need some time to connect within.' This is why getting up and moving around regularly, or meditating for five minutes every hour, is such a positive thing to do, especially if you know that you will be seated in front of a desk for protracted periods.

The integration of logic and reason with our deepest emotions can be difficult to navigate. The best thing you can do for your neck is to maintain its flexibility and range of movement. Massages, yoga and stretching are great ways to keep a good range of free movement in your neck.

If you are feeling confused around a certain issue, and are unsure whether to go with your heart or your head, allow yourself to sit in silence for a moment. Never try to resist pain or beliefs that are concerning you. Don't fight the feelings — simply breath into them. Breath into them and expand them. What I mean by this is: close your eyes and take three deep breaths. Feel into your neck and feel into any sensations you may be experiencing. And just observe. No judgement, just observation. If you feel stiffness, say to yourself 'stiffness here', and hone in on the stiff section of your neck.

Checklist and guidance for neck pain

- If you feel pain, locate the pain.
- Is the pain all over the neck or is it concentrated behind the base of the back of the head and neck?
- Is it a dull pain or an acute pain?
- Is the pain localised at one point?
- What does the stiffness or pain want you to do, do you think? Does it want you to adjust your head position? Does it want you to take a break and relax?
- Does it want a massage or a stretch?
- Is it trying to tell you something more, such as 'you need to be more flexible in this circumstance', 'you need to adjust your position on this matter' or 'you need to look around a little more and make a more informed decision'.

Ask your neck to direct you towards correct decision making. Remember that your neck forms the upper part of your spinal column and needs to be kept in alignment with your personal values and belief systems for it to function optimally.

If you're still finding it difficult to align your head and heart, ask yourself the following question: 'If I take this course of action am I coming from a place of fear or a place of love?' A place of love gives variations of correct answers and outcomes; a place of fear creates struggle, regret and difficulty.

THE THROAT

Moving inwards a little, still in the same region, is the throat and larynx. The throat and larynx play a major role in speaking, breathing and swallowing. If we look a little closer we see that this area is responsible for what we take in and how we express ourselves.

The throat serves as the gateway — by housing the mouth and oesophagus — to allow nutrients and liquids into your system. At a more symbolic level it could be seen as a gateway to allowing you to swallow or take in new ideas. The throat is actually quite a sensitive area and, along with the tonsils, is the first way you experience the world. Is there anything you're currently struggling to take in? Feel into your throat area next time you are taking on a new concept and see what it has to tell you. Does your throat constrict when you hear about something you don't like? Or is it relaxed?

In order to fully and freely express itself, the throat needs to feel relaxed and lubricated. The throat houses the vocal chords, which produce sounds for speech. The throat provides an avenue for expressing yourself creatively — through song, poetry and deliberate word choice. You can choose to hold back your thoughts or express them freely. The throat needs to project your message in a clear and forthright way. In order to do this, you need to feel conviction in the ideas you are wishing to express. If what you express is not in alignment with your head and heart, you will struggle to deliver your words. Remember again that the throat sits directly in between the head and heart. You may often experience a tug of war between your mind (wrapped in your ego) and your heart (connected to your soul). Words spoken from the heart will always have more impact than facts and figures delivered purely from the mind.

How many times have you fallen asleep during a lecture or class because the content was dry and boring? The content was there, but there was no passion in the delivery and you felt it. Next, think of a time when you had a lecturer or teacher who bounced into the room, excited to share their knowledge. They were so full of enthusiasm that they couldn't wait to share their content and it was contagious. This is what I mean by connecting the throat to both your head and heart. Think of singers that touch your soul with their song; they have connected their words to their emotions and relay them to their audience with purity and heartfelt expression.

Consider the ways you could express your ideas, thoughts and emotions in a loving and heartfelt way, that assists you to get the full impact of your message across. If you keep this idea in mind each time you are about to express yourself, you will find your communication becomes richer and more fluid, expressed with a deeper sense of beauty.

Finally, the throat and larynx function as a passageway to ensure the smooth delivery of air to the body. The connection between the sinus cavities and the throat allows full inhalation and exhalation of air. This area needs to be recognised for the vital role it plays on a moment-by-moment basis to keep us alive.

I've already stressed the importance of breathing in an earlier section, yet I mention it again here to remind you that the simple act of breathing can help centre you and give you a greater sense of peace and a stronger feeling of control and wellbeing. Things that seemed so out of control when you are holding your breath take on a different perspective when you finally stop to breathe. Breathing gives you what no amount of goal attainment can ever do… it gives you *clarity* and peace of mind. So please, take time to breath.

As a symbolic reminder of the importance of this area, I have included a section on scarf styling. A scarf can have an incredible impact on your outfit. It can turn casual streetwear into a stylish outfit that makes you stand out as someone who understands and communicates their sense of style.

As you learn each style, and every time somebody compliments you on your scarf — the way you wear it or the design or print — remind yourself to breath. Remind yourself that the ideas you express and take in need to be in alignment with your head and heart, and that if you're feeling stiffness in the neck, then perhaps it is time to take some time away from the computer. Give your neck a massage or book in for a yoga class to improve your flexibility and range of movement.

SCARVES AND SCARF STYLES

The addition of a scarf around your neck and décolletage adds a touch of class, versatility and elegance that can't be matched by many other accessories. The scarf also serves a practical purpose, providing warmth, modesty and protection. Its origins date all the way back to Ancient Egypt, where it is recorded as worn by Queen Nefertiti.

Famous fashion house designer Hermes popularised the scarf in Europe, and the advent of the Second world war meant the scarf in general, became a functional piece of attire in addition to a fashion accessory. For example, head scarves were used by women working in factories to keep their long hair out of the way. Advances in technology and textiles have meant that scarves — traditionally an expensive item — are now readily available. So we see scarves worn often, as an item that lifts an outfit from ho-hum to chic and classy.

When it comes to scarf styles, it is important to consider what area of the body you wish to add volume to (or not) first. Another aspect to consider is the size of the scarf you have to hand. Finally, you need to consider the fabric of your scarf.

> *Do you have a long neck and elongated décolletage?*

Some women have a lot of length from the chin to their bust line. Placing a scarf in this section can create the visual volume to nicely balance this shape.

If this is you, consider textured fabrics and ruffled designs in your scarf. Scarves that have more fabric (rather than less) will work to achieve this balance best.

Also consider scarf-tying styles that add bulk above the neckline and just under the chin. This adds visual width to an area of the body that is generally long (the neck).

Think voluminous knots. See how the first two styles add a lot of bulk to the neck and front of the chest. This effectively shortens the section visually. You do not want your scarf fabric to lie flat — you want it to create bulk. This causes our eyes to scan horizontally rather than vertically over those areas.

Do you want to add volume to the bust line?

Look for bulky knits. Scarves with ruffles and anything chunky that will create volume in the chest area. If the fabric is lightweight, ensure that there is plenty of fabric in the scarf to play with.

Even though you want to tie the scarf quite high around your neck, you also want to leave a tiny gap under the chin, so at least a hint of the throat is visible (unless you have a super long neck). Below are some examples of scarf styles that add bulk to the chest area.

Do you want to wear a scarf but you have a large bust or shorter neck?

Look for narrower scarves made of thinner fabrics that hang flat against your body. This stops the issue of too much extra bulk, created by the fuller fabric of certain scarf styles, in this area of the body.

Consider tying your scarf more loosely, and further down the décolletage. The lower the neck opening, the more the eye will travel down the chest and add visual length to the area, making it more slimming. Longer scarfs will work well for this area. Below are examples of loose-neck tied styles that work on larger busts.

On the left, we see the scarf is tied low and loosely, with the knot pushed to one side —asymmetrical placement creates a diagonal line. This draws the attention away from the main bulk of the bust line.

The next image shows a woman with the scarf just hanging around her neck and down the front of her body, creating slimming vertical lines down her front — this can be worn loose, or with a belt as seen here.

❦ Neck and Throat; Scarves and Scarf Styles ❧

Next, see how a thinner scarf works with a larger bust line. It hangs over the chest and gives a darker ensemble a pop of colour without adding bulk.

Or, simply create an infinity knot with your scarf and pull the opening down lower so that it elongates your décolletage.

Chapter 12

Face, Skin and Foundation

FACE and SKIN

Moving now to your face. Do you like what you see? Or are you staring at each pore with one of those magnifying mirrors, looking for every imperfection? Run your fingers over your face. Does your skin feel dry, oily, sensitive to the touch? Is your facial skin one even colour or do you have pigmentation and redness in sections? Is there congestion? Signs of aging? Is your skin radiant? Do you look in the mirror and say, 'Wow, look at you! Aren't you the cutest thing ever?' Looking at your face is the ideal time to work on your self-talk. Really listen to the comments that get thrown at yourself in the mirror. Is it possible that your inner voice could speak in a more loving way? Of course it could!

Let's explore how the face and the facial skin works. Facial muscles are innervated by the facial nerve, working to move the skin of the face. For example, the muscles around the mouth lift and lower the lips to open and close them for speech.

The facial muscles all work together to convey facial expressions or emotions while communicating face-to-face. This ability to convey emotion helps others to correctly interpret our intent or meaning, whether we are communicating verbally or non-verbally. Groups of tiny muscles in the face all work simultaneously to help us express our true feelings.

A study by Fritz Strack and colleagues, in 1988, showed how closely linked facial expressions and emotions are. The study followed two groups: each were asked to watch cartoons. They asked the first group to put a pen in their mouth between their teeth and their lips (forcing the face to smile) whilst watching a cartoon. The second group was asked to hold the pen only with their lips (preventing a smile).

What Fritz and his colleagues discovered was that the first group found the cartoons more humorous. These findings show that facial expressions generate feedback to the brain about the emotional state. Looks like your exercise instructor is on to something when they tell you to smile while you are exercising — even if you're about to pass out. It seems a smile will help you push through your discomfort and reframe your internal experience of the activity.

While your skin is the only barrier between you and your environment. Therefore, it needs to be given immense respect and attention. It is also extremely sensitive and delicate, as well as one of the first areas to demonstrate ageing.

The skin's main functions are:

1. Protection
   - Your skin has an *acid mantle* (with a pH of 5.5) made from sweat and oil (or sebum) and this mantle helps discourage the growth of bacteria and fungi.
   - Your skin also contains *melanin*, a pigment responsible for making the skin appear darker. Melanin also helps to protect your skin against UV (ultraviolet) rays.

2. Sensation
   - This includes the ability to feel heat, cold, sense of touch, pressure and pain.

3. Absorption
   - The skin on the face the skin is able to absorb certain facial ingredient preparations — look for *cosmeceutical grade products* if you want your products to create a demonstrable improvement to the skin health.

4. Vitamin D production
   - When sun comes in contact with the skin this produces a chemical reaction that creates Vitamin D. Between ten and

thirty minutes of sun exposure a few times a week is generally sufficient.

5. Regulation
   - Your blood vessels are continually dilating (expanding) and constricting (narrowing) in order to maintain a consistent body temperature of around 37 degrees Celsius.
   - Perspiration assists to keep your body cool.
   - Also, your fat cells (the subcutaneous layer of your skin) have insulating properties, helping to keep out the heat when it's warm or store heat when it's cold.

6. Excretion and Secretion
   - The skin has sweat glands that secrete fluid waste called perspiration- consisting water, urea, salts, sugars and ammonia. It also secretes oil (sebum).

As you can see, our skin is an important component of our body. It is in fact our largest body organ. Skin functions as a protective mechanism, one that breathes and sheds on a regular basis. Every 21–28 days your skin sends new cells to the surface. As this body part is a living, breathing organism, it needs to be attended in order to thrive. Each of us possesses a unique skin type that needs to be treated in individual ways. For example, if you have an oilier skin type, you will need to follow a different skin regime than someone with a dry skin type. Regular cleansing, exfoliation, hydration, treatment and protection is required for every skin type.

Healthy, glowing skin is definitely an asset that women need to concentrate on maintaining. Skin is sensitive, and is a great indicator of how we are travelling emotionally and hormonally. You tend to get pimples on the chin when you're ovulating (almost like upside down devil's horns), or hormonal stress pimples around the jaw line (these are larger pimples that don't really have a head) when you're under a lot of stress or pressure.

The skin is an amazing barometer of what is going on internally. You only need to look at the skin around the eyes after having no sleep to show just how sensitive it is, and how important it is to look after your wellbeing. The sensitive nature of skin means it will tell you if it doesn't like a particular food or environment, by breaking out in hives or a rash. Pay attention to your skin and it will reward you with a healthy glow. Ignore it and watch it flare up — until you start paying attention.

To gain maximum radiance your skin will benefit most from a disciplined skincare regime.

This includes:

- Daily cleansing, morning and night. This process will remove pollutants, makeup, oil and dirt build-up, and will ensure your skin remains healthy.

- Exfoliating your skin with a scrub or enzyme-based mask, 1–3 times per week.

Exfoliation can be either physical or chemical. An example of a physical exfoliant, that you can use at home, is a facial scrub. A physical exfoliant works by manually abrading the top layer of skin. For a deeper exfoliation treatment, you could go to a skincare clinic or salon, and have a microdermabrasion treatment, this is an example of a professional skin treatment that uses physical exfoliation.

An example of a chemical exfoliation that you can use at home is an enzyme-based mask. Enzymes work by eating away the dead skin cells which, once removed, reveal healthier, brighter skin. For a deeper chemical exfoliation treatment at a skin clinic or salon, a chemical peel or an enzyme peel would be used.

- Using a skin serum on a daily basis (or as recommended) prior to moisturising.

  A skin serum (or booster or concentrate) is a concentrated skin-care product that targets a particular skin concern. For example, your concern might be pigmentation. In this case, you would look for a serum that has brightening, antioxidant properties, such as Vitamin C. This treatment product would give you the best results.

  If you've ever had a facial, you may have been asked whether you wanted an infusion of some sort of booster, which would have either been massaged into your skin or pushed deeper into the skin with electrical equipment. If you had a deep exfoliation treatment beforehand, this will have assisted the booster to penetrate your skin.

- Using a moisturiser day and night, with a blend of hydrating and nourishing ingredients, depending on your skin type. You may choose to wear a lighter moisturiser during the day and a more nourishing moisturiser overnight. This is completely dependent on the oil levels of your skin, as well as your personal preference.

- A facial mask 1–2 times per week. A facial mask is similar to a booster, as it is also a product that targets particular skin conditions, such as breakouts, dehydration or pigmentation. After using this product, you should have brighter, cleaner or rehydrated skin, depending on the type of mask.

- Wear sunscreen daily. Try to find a sunscreen that includes antioxidants in its ingredient listing, as this will provide added protection for your skin.

Here is a list of ingredients to look out for in skin care that can be beneficial:

- Vitamin C has great brightening and anti-ageing properties.

- Hyaluronic Acid has exceptional moisture binding properties and is, therefore, excellent for maintaining the skin hydration.

- Alpha Hydroxy Acids (AHAs) work to breakdown the bonds between dead skin cells, revealing fresher, healthier skin.

- Antioxidants protect the skin from free radical damage, pollution and UV exposure.

There are other anti-ageing, calming, acne-clearing ingredients that have not been mentioned here. However, those mentioned will improve skin health for all.

Your face — including your facial skin — is the place where people direct their attention when engaging you in conversation. Having clarity and radiance in the skin will help you shine your light and build connection with others. If you have been hiding your true feelings and not connecting authentically, your face will show signs of stress or strain. On the flip side, the more excitement and joy you express around a particular situation, the more your face lights up or glows. A healthy, radiant glow will turn many heads, and will draw people to you.

FOUNDATION

Another way to enhance the skin, at a surface level, is through the application of foundation. Foundation isn't meant to be a mask used to hide behind; it is designed to even out your skin tone. Ensure your foundation matches your actual skin tone. This can be achieved by placing a small amount along your jawline and onto your neck. This will give you an accurate match, as the skin on your neck rarely sees the sun.

A variety of tools can be used for application, including: freshly washed hands, a foundation brush, a kabuki brush or a beauty blender. Or you can use a combination of these items.

Foundation Application

Before applying foundation it's important to properly prepare your skin by:

1. Ensuring the skin is clean and, if you've just stepped out of a hot shower, has cooled down.
2. Applying a hydration mist.
3. Applying moisturiser. Using one that has sunscreen included is great during the day.
4. If the skin is rough in any areas, such as lips, cheeks or nose, applying a thicker balm on these sections of the face.
5. Applying primer and buffing or pressing this into the skin. The main function of primer is to minimise fine lines and pores, and to increase the longevity of your foundation throughout the day, by controlling the oils in the skin.
6. Applying eyeshadow primer over your eyelid area.

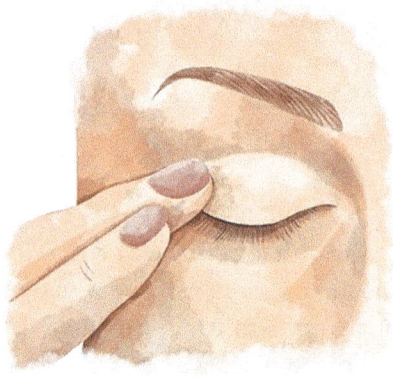

Once you have thoroughly prepared your skin, you are now ready for foundation application.

7. Using foundation that perfectly matches your skin, decide on the tool you wish to use to blend your foundation into your skin. You will gain best results by applying the foundation with one tool, then buffing it into the skin with another tool. Buffing foundation into your skin will also help your makeup to last longer. Remember that

thin layers of foundation, slowly built up to the level of coverage you desire always looks better than one thick layer of foundation. It's similar to painting your nails with a few thinner coats. You achieve coverage either way, but one appears smooth and even and the other just looks ... not-classy. Foundation, applied well, should still look like skin, simply more even in tone.

If you choose to use your hands to apply your foundation, remember to spread and then press or pat it into the skin. You can then use a damp sponge or buffing brush to achieve a more polished finish.

If you choose a foundation brush, use gentle strokes, with the brush sitting flat against the skin, as much as possible. Again, this is similar to the way you would apply nail polish. If your brush is flat when you apply nail polish, you'll achieve a smoother application, whereas if your brush is perpendicular, you will have less control. This exact same principle applies with foundation application.

Once you have applied and spread the foundation onto your skin, you can push the makeup further into your skin by using stippling movements (bouncing the brush against your skin) with your foundation brush. No additional product needs to be used during this process. You can then grab either a damp sponge (a beauty blender) or a blending brush, and buff the skin to remove any excess foundation sitting on the skin's surface. This will help you create foundation coverage that looks like a second skin, rather than a layer of cakey grease paint.

8. Double check your foundation application by looking over the following areas:
   (i) The hairline. Is your foundation blended in properly to the hairline? If not, you can end up with a very distinct line of where you stopped your foundation application.
   (ii) The eyebrows. Is there a distinct line between your foundation and the skin just before the tops of your brows?
   (iii) The ears. The ears make up part of your face, so ignoring them when applying foundation means that you could end up with white ears and a golden beige face.
   (iv) The jawline. Blending is everything when it comes to a successful skin foundation application. If you stop your foundation application at your jawline and chin, you will often have harsh lines and strong colour differences between the face, the neck and the décolletage.
9. Once you've looked over these sections, grab a blending brush and, with any remaining foundation, blend over these areas so that you have a more harmonious finish.

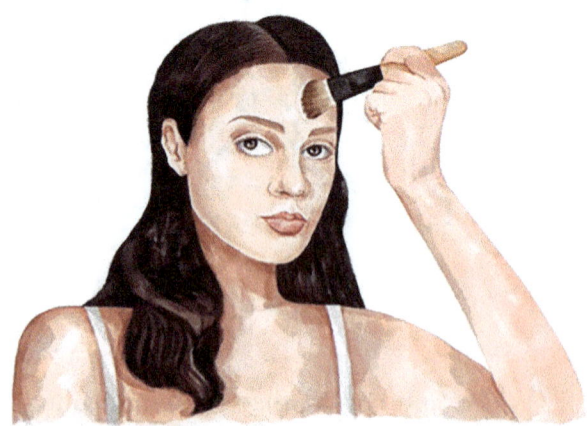

10. Apply concealer in a shade that matches your foundation, to brighten the under-eye area if needed. You can apply this by spreading your foundation from the inner corners of the eyes and

patting it underneath the eyes following along the orbital bone (around the under-eye bone) with your ring fingers or a concealer brush. Once again, buff the concealer to stop it from caking.

11. Look back over your base for any creases in the eyelids or under the eyes, and pat them out with your fingers.
12. Apply translucent or matching skin-coloured powder to these finer areas immediately. Ensure you apply your powder with a smaller, fluffier brush around these delicate, hard-to-reach areas. Next, apply powder to the t-zone (the centre of the forehead, sides of nose and chin). You can stop there with your powder coverage if you want a dewy, healthy skin glow finish. For a more matte finish, use either a translucent powder or a pressed skin-toned powder all over the skin, applied with a jumbo powder brush in criss-cross motions, or pushed into the skin with a powder puff. (Powder puff application has more longevity.)
13. Apply setting spray to finish. This will seal your makeup, allowing your foundation to last longer.

Chapter 13

Lips, Nose, Cheekbones

THE LIPS

> 'Lips are the most sensual organ we are allowed to expose.'
> — *Anonymous*

Take a close look at your facial features. Start by examining your lips, which help you to express yourself through words and song. Lips are sensual by nature. Through the kiss —whether romantic or familiar — the lips provide a more intimate way of connecting than a simple shake of the hand.

A kiss on the cheek enables us to enter another's personal space and create an immediate sense of intimacy, while the impact of a lover's kiss has been documented in love poem after love poem, for centuries. It cannot be denied that the kiss brings us closer to our loved ones, so keeping our lips soft and sensuous is essential.

Our lips are also smile-makers or frown-makers. A smile will add volume to your cheeks. It is the ultimate de-ager! A frown, on the other hand, will increase wrinkles specific to this area, called marionette lines. These lines give the face a downturned expression, making you seem sad or angry.

I'll admit that you are more prone to crow's feet (wrinkles around your eyes) when you smile more but, ultimately, ageing will happen to us all. And the imprint created by many smiles is far more attractive and radiant — and, by association, youthful — than too many frowns.

Lips, Nose, Cheekbones

The simple act of a gentle smile helps to soften your facial muscles and automatically sends feedback to the brain that will elevate your mood. Due to the magnificent impact of mirror neurons in our brains, when you smile it also causes recipient or recipients of the smile to feel happy. A smile creates a sense of joy, warmth and beauty for the wearer, as well as a sense of welcome for the recipient.

> 'A smiling face is a beautiful face. A smiling heart is a happy heart.' *Dr T.P. Chia*

Another function of the lips is that they serve as an entry point for nourishment; they have an important function while eating, including holding food and manoeuvring it into the mouth. They're necessary in the act of drawing in liquids and they enable us to chew and swallow with our mouths closed.

Lips help us to whistle, and any musician who plays a wind instrument, such as a saxophone, flute or trumpet, will understand how essential their lips are in producing the necessary blowing sounds required to generate music.

A person who is hearing impaired pays close attention to another person's lips to assist them to use the cues provided by the lips, teeth and tongue, in order to understand the words being spoken. The lips are an important factor in the articulation of sound and speech; they are essential in enabling us to round our vowels, for example. Audrey Hepburn was quoted as saying, 'For attractive lips, speak words of kindness.'

Take a moment to remember the kind words and praise you have offered to yourself or to others today.

- How would you rate your lip attractiveness — according to Audrey Hepburn's definition?
- Were there kinder words or praises that you could have spoken?
- What nutrients did you allow to pass by your lips today? Could you have made better choices?
- How much of your day was spent with a smile on your face?
- How much of your day was spent wearing a frown?

- How welcoming and warm were you today?
- How many kisses did you give to others?
- Were the words you chose to use spoken from the heart? Or were they less sincere, more a case of 'lip service'?

Who would have thought that lips could be so significant? Yet they are. Now, to enhance them aesthetically, I have a couple of tips to help you create the perfect pout.

Firstly, if you want perfect lipstick application you require a smooth base. If you run your fingers over your lips and they feel dry and chapped, here are a couple of very quick and easy home remedies for you to create with items generally found in a kitchen pantry. (You won't have to hunt down obscure items from exotic location for this!)

Homemade Lip scrub recipe

Ingredients

- ½ tsp of sugar
- ½ tsp Olive Oil
- ½ tsp of honey (optional)

Method

Mix ingredients together in a small bowl.

Application

Apply this mixture in circular motions, either with a spare toothbrush or your fingertip. The sugar works to exfoliate the lips while the olive oil (and optional honey) hydrate the lips.

Now apply your favourite lip balm and pat it fully into your lips with your fingers until the balm dissolves. Dab off any excess balm prior to applying your lipstick.

Perfect Red Lipstick Application

Lip liner

Many people question whether lip liner is even required. Admittedly, it is not crucial or essential, particularly now that many matte and long-wear lipsticks are available. However, there are a few of the reasons why lip liners are still popular, and it's because they can help with the following issues:

1) Lip liner helps to prevent bleeding or feathering of lipstick — this is especially important if you choose to wear red lipstick — as its formulation has a waxy, long-lasting base.

2) If you wear a satin or creamy-textured lipstick, lip liner provides a base (similar to primer for foundation) for your lipstick. Your lipstick will last longer and will stay on more evenly. When the entire lip is filled in with lip liner this provides a coloured base that remains, even when the lipstick wears off.

3) Lip liners help to define, shape and correct your lip line. For example, if your top lips are uneven, a lip liner pencil is easier to work with as a corrector tool than your actual lipstick.

Now that you understand the importance of lip liner, I will provide a step-by-step guide about how to apply it in the best possible way.

STEP 1: Sharpen your pencil! Having a sharp pencil will give you more precision with your lip liner application.

STEP 2: Place the pinky finger of the hand you'll be applying your lip liner with onto your chin. This will provide stability, enabling you to keep your hands steady while creating a precision lip line.

STEP 3: Place a mark at the apex of your cupid's bow, then draw down to the centre of the lip. Repeat on the other side. This will provide an even V shape across the top of your cupid's bow.

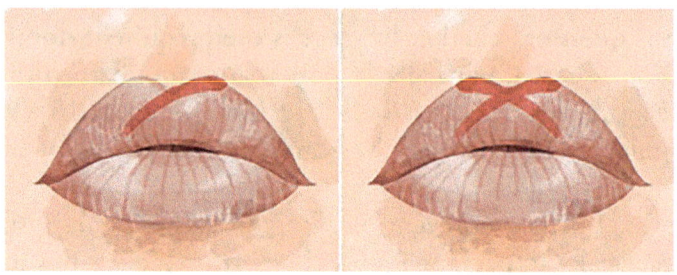

STEP 4: Line the base of your lower lip — just the section that sits directly beneath your cupid's bow — dragging your pencil along sideways.

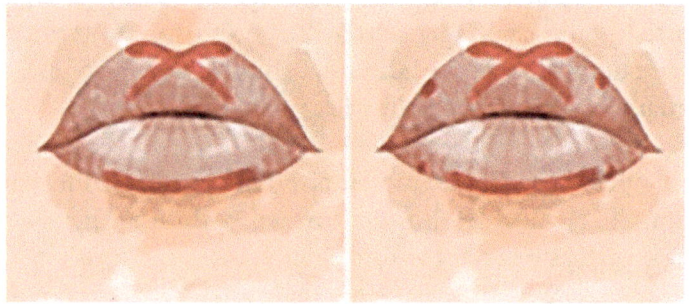

STEP 5: Line the outer corners of your top lips, pulling the pencil upwards towards the outside edge of the cupid's bow.

STEP 6: Fill in any gaps between the outer edge of the cupids bow and the outside edge of the lips. Repeat on the other side.

STEP 7: Draw lip liner from the outer corner of the bottom lip and drag the pencil down towards the edge of the line you created at the base of the lips in STEP 4. Repeat on the other side.

STEP 8: Optional step — fill in lips with lip liner.

STEP 9: Check to see whether your lips need to be corrected anywhere, in order to appear even and balanced.

Applying your lipstick

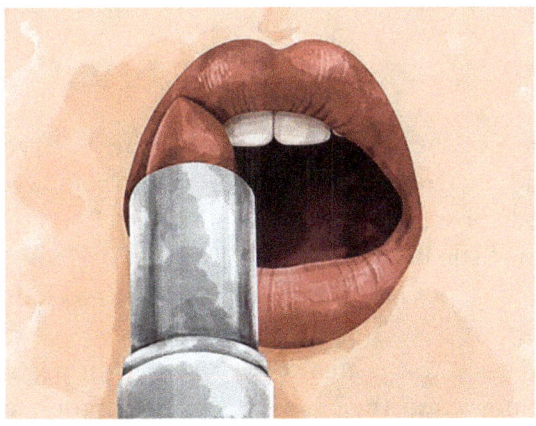

Once you have gone through the above steps with your lip liner, the hard work has been done. If you want colour intensity in one hit, you can now simply apply your lipstick straight out of the bullet. If you want greater longevity, use a lip brush. Commence at the bottom lip, pushing the product back and forth across the lower lip with your brush. Then, drag the lipstick up from the outer corner of the top lip towards the cupid's bow and repeat on the other side. Now, drag your lipstick from the outer bottom lip corner down towards the base of the lower lip line and repeat on the other side. Smack your lips together for a more even distribution of lip colour. All the while, do your best to stay inside the lines you have created.

Cleaning up your edges

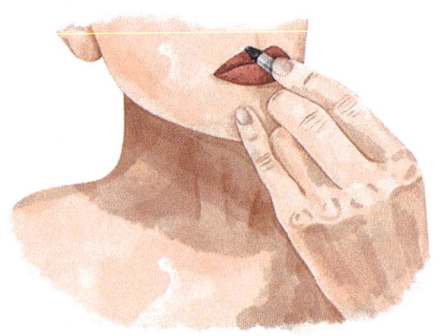

Sometimes, you'll find yourself going out of the lines, especially with red lipstick. You were doing so well and then your phone rang — now perfection has a wobbly edge. Not to worry, it's nothing that a concealer in a colour that matches your skin tone and a fine brush can't fix. Simply apply this to the outer edges of your lipline for a flawless finish.

You look beautiful! Blow yourself a kiss.

THE NOSE

We're moving now to the nose. Have a look at the nose you've been given. Is it balanced and centered? When you breathe through your nose, is your breath steady and constant or is it short and quick? Feel the warmth of the air as it tickles the little hairs (cilia) that line the inside of your nose as you breathe in and out. Does one nostril appear to be working better than the other? Or are they working together harmoniously?

Pay close attention to the area at the base of your nostrils, where the air first enters your nose, and then feel the warm sensation at the base of the nostrils, just above the lip line, where the air hits as it is exhaled through the nose. Why should you do this? Concentrating your attention on this point is a meditation technique used by Vipassana to help maintain your mind's focus. Focusing on your breath encourages you to focus on the here and now, not on possible futures (which can cause high levels of anxiety), nor on the past (which can lead to a sense of depression or regret).

Too often we become caught up in our mind, either repeating scenarios from the past that we wish were otherwise or projecting into the future and anticipating the worst. Essentially, we are wishing our lives away and ignoring the gift of the present moment.

Is it any wonder that your nose holds such a central and prominent position on your face?

Your nose is not asking you to criticise it when you look in the mirror. It is better to use that glance at your nose as a reminder to return to the here and now, through a concentrated focus on the breath.

Please stop wishing that your nose was skinnier, less pointy, not so hooked, less turning up, less turning down. The list goes on and on ... to the benefit of the plastic surgeon's bank account! If this is you, please start your day by looking in the mirror and giving gratitude to the nose you have, for enabling the process of inhalation and providing you with life-giving oxygen. It's a bit of a big deal!

Another biggie is that your nose permits you to smell the air. It allows you to take in all of the aromas (good and bad) that your environment has to offer. This ability to smell gives life greater richness. It also helps you to sense danger (the smell of smoke alerts us to something burning) and to recognise the smell of putrefaction from food that has gone off — before you put it in your mouth! Thank you, nose.

According to studies, your sense of smell becomes sharper with exercise. Our sense of smell is also strongly connected to our sense of taste. It is important to pay attention to how certain smells make you feel, as your sense of smell is connected to your limbic system (this is the part of the brain connected to your emotions and emotional memory). The perfume industry, and even the food industry, understand just how important the association of a particular fragrance or smell is to how we feel about a person, a place, or a food item that carries a particular scent.

Aromatherapy is the inhalation or bodily application of fragrant essential oils for therapeutic purposes: the use of aroma to enhance a feeling of wellbeing. You only need to see how quickly a child settles when they have a few drops of lavender essential oil applied to a tissue near their pillow. Conversely, essential oils such as rosemary are said to improve focus and concentration. There is a huge world of 'scentual' pleasure that our nose enables us to experience. Another reason to have appreciation and respect for that nose of yours.

Additionally, your nose works as a filtration system, assisting to filter and warm the air before it enters your respiratory system. At the back of the nose are lumps of tissue called the adenoids, which help to fight infection if bacteria enters the system. This is why the area around your nose swells when you become sick.

Your nose also acts an instinctual barometer. It's your nose that registers social welcome or the presence of tension, chemistry, danger, or something being … not quite right. 'I smell a rat!' This ability is strongly connected to what is better known as our animal instinct. As it holds the most prominent and central part on the face, the nose has had a number of sayings attached to it:

— 'Keep your nose clean', meaning stay out of trouble.
— 'Get your nose out of other peoples' business.'
— 'He had a nose for it', meaning he had a natural flair or instinct for it.

The more you show gratitude for your nose's functions, the more you will start to appreciate its true value, how much it adds to life's richness through the sense of smell, through enabling you to access memories simply by inhaling the air around you, transporting you back to significant or cherished moments in time. There's a reason we are often told: 'remember to stop and smell the roses'. There is a richness to your immediate environment that you won't notice if you don't allow yourself time to pause. The more you can pause in life, the more you open yourself up to receiving. The more you let your nose guide you, the more your intuitive abilities will kick in.

So, please take the time to breathe — whether it's through yoga, meditation or conscious breathing throughout the day — and watch how your energy changes and expands. You'll find yourself being more grounded, present and aware of what's really happening in your environment as a consequence. And your life will take on a greater richness as a result.

Now that we understand how significant our noses are, let's see how we can show it some love at the physical level.

Lips, Nose, Cheekbones

The nose is the central part of your T-Zone — comprised of your forehead, nose and chin — and this area of your face is generally oilier than other areas. As a consequence, you may find more open pores, blackheads and shine (due to oil flow) along the nose. Therefore a great way to maintain this area of the face is to give yourself a mini T-zone facial once a month.

Mini T-zone facial

Steam your skin by placing your head over hot water (not in it). It is optional, but beneficial, to add a couple of drops of a purifying essential oil, such as lemon. Steam for 1–5 minutes.

Creating your own purifying clay mask:

Ingredients

1. Approximately 1–2 tablespoons of clay per application. There are different clays for different skin types and concerns. These include:
   — *Bentonite & Fullers Earth Clay* for oily skin, due to its high oil absorption properties.
   — *Kaolin Clay* for gentle exfoliation effect. (Kaolin clay is great for most skins wanting a smoothing or brightening effect.)
   — *French green clay* for a combination of oil absorption and gentle exfoliation. This type of clay is best for normal to oily skin types.

2. Purifying essential oils are always optional, but those you can mix into the mask include:
   — lemon
   — tea tree
   — geranium
   — lavender

   One or two drops will suffice.

3. 1–2 teaspoons of water — until the clay becomes a paste.

Method

Once you have all your ingredients ready, mix them in a small bowl. Add the water slowly and mix until you have a smooth paste. The consistency should be thin enough to apply to the skin without dragging, but not so thin that it dribbles down the face.

Application

Apply to the T-zone if this is your main area of concern. This mask is also great for refining the appearance of blackheads on the nose. Alternatively, it can be used all over the face, neck and décolletage.

You can be fancy, if you like, and use a brush to apply your mask, or you can simply apply it with your fingers.

Leave for 10–15 minutes. You'll know when the clay is ready to be removed because it will begin to harden. This is your mask's indicator that it is ready to come off. Remove with a warm, wet face cloth.

Once the mask is thoroughly removed there is an Asian facial technique that does an amazing job of closing off the pores. Fill a bowl with cold water and add a few blocks of ice, to help make the water as cold as possible. Cup your hands in the water and throw it over your face 50–100 times. I don't know why it has to be that number, but it works.

Finish with your favourite serum and hydrating lotion or moisturizer. Your nose will sparkle and love you for paying it such special attention.

THE CHEEKBONES

Shift your focus to your cheekbones, which support your mouth and eyes to smile. Are your cheeks plump, chiselled, boney or hollow? If you pinch them, do they bounce back? Is there a natural rosiness to them or are they a little sallow? Please try to just observe, rather than judge.

Have you noticed that public speakers need a lot of water? If you are talking non-stop, you'll notice the need to replenish your mouth with water. This is because cheek cells secrete a continuous supply of something called mucin. Mucin is the main element of mucous. This, in combination with saliva, helps to maintain a moist environment in the mouth. In other words, your cheeks act as the lubricators of your mouth and help you to talk for hours on end. Thank you, cheeks! What would we do without them?

Cheeks also help during the process of chewing. The combined effort of the cheeks and tongue help to keep food between the teeth.

Are your cheeks feeling tight from smiling and laughter? The more you notice them on a daily basis, the more moments of joy you're experiencing; the cheeks are major players in the expression of a beaming smile.

There is even a name for the smile that uses both the lips and the cheeks, rather than the lips-only smile, which is considered insincere. It's called the 'Duchenne Smile'. Katrina Schmidt, a vocal coach and performer, says that by singing with a Duchenne smile, which causes cheekbones to rise, a bigger space is created within the mouth that helps your singing voice resonate. She also explains that singing with a smile on your face improves the lightness and quality of your vocal tone. 'A brighter timbre helps the voice project into a room and improves the understandability of words.'

With this in mind, could placing a smile on your face when talking improve your ability to be understood? Could the mumblers of the world benefit from doing this? Could your ability to connect, be clearly understood and project your words be solved with the simple act raising your cheeks and smiling?

Why not try it for a week and see if your relationships and communication with others improves? I'm positive it won't hurt to smile a little more with those gorgeous cheeks. I'm sure that's the main reason they came to be on your face.

Now that we've discovered how essential your cheeks are in the processes of eating, laughing and talking, let's look at ways that we can show these beauties off to the world through makeup.

How to contour, highlight and apply blush

If you feel that your cheekbones need emphasising, or you just feel as though you need a little colour or pick-me-up in the face, then contouring, highlighting and blush application is for you.

Contouring

Contouring adds the dimension of shade to the face. Why would you want a darker colour underneath your cheeks, you may ask? It's because darkness adds depth. Your eye pushes back the dark area; therefore, if you feel your cheeks are too chubby, contouring is a great way to cut through the roundness of the cheek and add dimension to the face. Essentially, it has a slimming effect on the cheeks.

NB: If you feel as though your cheekbones are making you look a little drawn, or if you're a person who loses weight easily from their face and wants to add more cheek, then ignore this section on contouring.

Otherwise, proceed with the following steps:

How to Contour

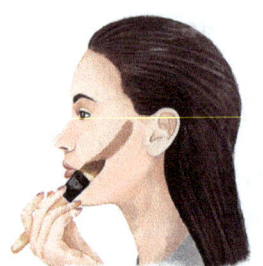 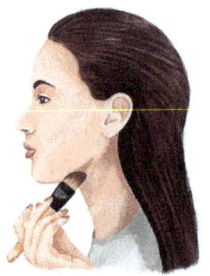 

Find the hollow area under your cheek bone with your finger. This is where your contour colour needs to go.

Choose a shade that's two or three shades darker than your natural skin tone, and apply the colour from the outer edge of the hollow of your cheekbone to the base of the cheekbone —this normally ends approximately 1–2 finger widths away from the edge of your nose. Then, blend. A severe line looks like a severe line, not like a naturally contoured cheek.

You can contour using a cream contour, a powder contour or a cream base that you cover with a powder of a similar colour. However you choose to apply your contour, remember that it's essential to blend the colour well.

Any remaining contour colour that remains on your brush can be applied to the base of the corner of the jawline, towards the chin, as well as to the temples of your forehead.

Once you're satisfied that your colour has been well blended, you can now move on to blush application.

Choosing your perfect shade of blush

Finding the right colour blush is an essential part of the process. If you have red hair and hazel or green eyes, then a bright pink blush won't do you any favours. If this is you, consider peachy tones, corals or terracottas. You want to choose a blush that is warm in colour or has a reddy-orange base to it rather than a pink-blue base.

If you already have redness in the cheeks — through broken capillaries, for example — then stick to terracotta tones. This will provide colour on your cheeks without intensifying the flushed look you may currently have.

If you have blonde hair, blue eyes and look great in pastels, then blue-based pink colours will look great on your cheeks.

The most important consideration is whether your skin has a warm tone or a cool tone. Once you know this, assess the depth of colour in your skin and hair. The deeper the skin colour, or the greater the difference between light and dark in your colouring, the deeper shade of colour you'll require. If there is very little difference between your skin colour and your hair colour, then you will be looking for softer colours, such as muted pinks or lighter versions of the colour you like.

Always match your blush colour to your lipstick colour. It doesn't have to be a perfect colour match, it just has to be a tone match of either a cool tone or a warm tone.

For more information on choosing the correct colours for your skin tone, see **Chapter 18**.

Blush application

Once you've found a colour you like, it is time to apply it to your cheeks. Try to keep a minimal amount of colour on your blush brush, remembering that you can always add more.

First, smile. It's best to smile when applying blush, as it highlights the actual zygomaticus (cheek muscle) that you are aiming to add colour to.

☙ When Glamour Meets Gratitude ❧

Next, dip your blush brush into your preferred shade of blush and tap off any excess. Now, create an imaginary boundary for your blush application — no further inwards (i.e. towards your nose) than the base of the centre of the coloured section of your eye. This is the section on your cheek where you will commence your blush application. You will then work and blend your blush upwards and outwards, in the direction towards your ear, along your cheek.

The majority of the pigment should sit on the cheek itself. If you feel you have applied too much blush or that the contour colour and the blush aren't blended well, you can always use a large, clean brush to blend the two together.

Highlighting the cheeks

Finally, in order to add a highlight to the cheekbones, it is worth finding a cream or powder with an iridescent quality. Choose a warm or cool shade

Lips, Nose, Cheekbones

according to your personal skin tone. To apply this, you will need either a fan brush or a small, fluffy brush or your fingertip.

You can apply the highlight colour prior to or after applying your blush. This will either make your highlight a final touch (after) or something that blends into the cheek as a whole (before). It really is a case of personal preference when it comes to the order of highlight application.

If you are using a cream highlighter, your finger is probably the best option for application, as the warmth of your fingertip will heat up the cream and make it easier to blend.

Start by finding the outer edge of the bone on the outer edge of the eye socket. You can apply your highlight from this point, bringing it along the top outer section of the cheek. You really don't want to bring it in any further than the outer edge of the coloured section of your eye.

The same rules apply if you are using powder and applying it with a fan brush or small, fluffy brush.

Either way, remember that it's better to use a small amount of highlight rather than having it dominate your makeup. Build your highlight application gently — we don't need to see you from the moon.

Chapter 14

Eyes, Ears and Brows

THE EYES

Take a close look into your eyes. What colour are they? Are they green? Are they a dark brown that almost resembles black? Or brown with yellow or auburn specks? Are they hazel with green specks or yellow specks? Are they blue? Deep blue or crystal clear blue? Are they grey but turn bluer or greener depending on the colour of top you wear?

Understanding your eye colour and its depth or clarity, as well as the secondary colours that sit within the iris (the coloured part of your eyes) will help you select eye shadows, lipsticks and clothing that enhance your colouring.

Look a little deeper. Are your eyes shining with joy or hollow with sadness? If the shiny sparkle isn't present, what do you need to bring back into your life? What are the things that create joy in your life? Are the muscles around the eyes soft and relaxed or tight and twitching? Are you allowing yourself sufficient periods of rest, or are you working and worrying so hard that everything is becoming strained? How could you create a better sense of balance between rest and work?

When your eyes are wide open what are they noticing? The eyes are constantly capturing images and then converting them into electronic signals to the brain, creating what we have come to take for granted as our sense of sight. According to R.N Clark https://clarkvision.com/imagedetail/eye-resolution.html, the human eye captures 300 megapixels of visual information every second.

Fortunately, a small section of the brain called the Reticular Activating System (RAS) filters all this information according to what is most relevant to your thoughts, beliefs, and needs, otherwise your senses would be overwhelmed.

Because of the RAS, however, when you pay attention to something you notice it more. If you're asked to look at all the red objects in a room, then they are what you will observe. It's worth remembering this when you have a preconceived idea about a person: if you believe that they are good, bad, clever or stupid then your RAS will show you evidence of that belief. What other thoughts could you be choosing that would enable you to see a more beautiful reality?

Close your eyes and notice how you are better able to 'go within' and be with your inner thoughts. This is something to consider doing when your head is too busy or you have an important decision to make. It is with your eyes closed that you are not only better able to quieten the mind but also to connect more closely with your heart and yourself.

It's ironic that for most people their strongest personal symbols are revealed through dreams, behind closed eyes. Dreams are a goldmine of symbolic interpretation. They reveal a great deal of the inner workings of the mind and reflect your feelings about situations that may not even come up on the radar of your logical mind.

But eyes are beautiful when they're open as well. They allow you to participate fully in your day-to-day life. The eyes are extremely expressive. If you could no longer talk, smile, or move the muscles of your face, your eyes would still be able to speak for you — possibly in a more intimate and authentic way.

Eye contact fosters better connections and greater honesty, and generally enriches relationships. Intimate, loving relationships are created by eye contact. One reason for this is that we express so many of our emotions both through and with the muscles around the eyes.[1] One study found that couples in love looked into each other's eyes 75% of the time during conversation, compared to 30–60% of those not in an intimate relationship. By maintaining eye contact with your partner, or the person you are listening to, you are indicating that they have your full attention.

---

[1] Susan Krausse Whitbourne

I don't know about you, but I prefer to interact with people who give me their full undivided attention.

The study also found that maintaining good eye contact while communicating made the message more memorable. The reason for this is that memory impressions and eye contact are strongly connected[2]. Essentially, if you want better and more connected relationships, it appears that there is plenty of research to back up the notion that looking at people when they are talking works. Couple good eye contact with a powerful smile and you'll have an incredible impact in your love life, at work and with people in general. *Rubin, Zick. "Lovers and Other Strangers: The Development of Intimacy in Encounters and Relationships: Experimental Studies of Self-Disclosure between Strangers at Bus Stops and in Airport Departure Lounges Can Provide Clues about the Development of Intimate Relationships." American Scientist, vol. 62, no. 2, 1974, pp. 182–190. JSTOR, www.jstor.org/stable/27844813. 2020.*

But there is a fine line between good eye contact and being too intense with your eye attention. Research from the University of Paris suggests that prolonged eye contact makes people more self-aware and more sensitive to their own thoughts, feelings and behaviours. Think of how you feel when a potential love interest holds your gaze.

Your eyes, regardless of whether they are the wrong colour, not big enough, too big, too baggy or too far apart, are what enable you to interpret the world around you visually and with clarity. When somebody is furious, the pressure builds behind their eyes. They 'see red'! Their anger becomes more intense and poor decisions and actions are often made. Loving energy, on the other hand, releases tension around the eyes and allows your gaze to soften. When your gaze is more gentle, you'll find that you perceive things less judgmentally and more clearly, be they people, objects or circumstances.

Sandy Newbigging, creator of the Mind Calm technique, explains that in order to be truly present one must make the effort to look ahead while maintaining an awareness of one's peripheral vision (similar to what's required of you when you are driving). This simple technique keeps the racing mind quiet and keeps your awareness in the present without much effort other than the use of your full vision. Next time you're finding that

---

[2] Research findings of a joint study between University of Wolverhampton and the University of Stirling.

your mind is judging too harshly, or running at 1000 miles per hour, take the time to use your full range of vision and notice the difference.

Being truly present is one of the keys to true happiness and contentment. A happy and loving heart shines through happy, loving eyes. Being truly present with your vision will allow you to fully take in life while creating a gentler, soft, radiant energy that attracts more positive people and experiences into your life.

Now that you understand more about your eyes and the loving focus technique, I invite you to consider techniques you can use when applying your eye makeup.

Eye shadow Tips

This section will teach you how to get the most out of your eye shadow palette. Many people use 1–3 colours and leave it at that. Instead, you should blend your colours so that you utilise as much of the palette as possible.

This is what you will normally find in an eye shadow palette.

- A skin tone colour for the entire eyelid area.
- A darker colour to enhance the eyelid crease.
- A mid-tone colour. These 'boring' mid-tones may seem unnecessary. However, the more you use them in your eyelid crease line the more graduated and professional your eye makeup will look. Instead of having a definite edge from using only a darker colour in the crease line, lay the mid-toned colour first for a seamless blend.
- Metallic, glittery or pearlescent colours are to be applied to the moveable lid. To achieve the most intensity from these eye shadows you can add a very small amount of setting spray (or water) to your brush before dipping it into the colour in your palette. Alternatively, you can apply concealer to the area first.
- Finally, a lighter matte or metallic colour can be added just below the brow line or to the inner corners of the eyes.

THE BROWS

Brows play a vital role in framing and shaping the eyes. When the eyebrows are well groomed, they can lift, soften and frame our eyes. Well-shaped brows also mean that you won't require as much makeup in order to look smart.

Why do these two hairy arched lines sit above our eyes anyway? Eyebrows have two main functions. First, they keep water and sweat out of your eyes. The natural arch of the brow and the direction of eyebrow hair growth divert moisture to the sides of the face, keeping the eye area free of sweat or moisture. This keeps your vision clear when, for example, you are caught in the rain or have been exercising.

Eyebrows also play a part in non-verbal communication. Body language experts, after careful analysis of the micro expressions of the face, have noted the following subtle movements of the eyebrows and what they convey. A *single raised eyebrow* can express skepticism ('Really?' 'You sure about that?') or interest ('Tell me more!').

How much of your day has been spent in discontentment, uncertainty or confusion? What will it take to take the furrow out of your brow? Is there something that you need to investigate further? Were you taken by surprise? How could you have been better prepared?

The eyebrows are as expressive as the eyes. Knowing how to embellish these beauties is a handy skill. There are many methods of shaping or filling in the brows:

- Tweezing
- Waxing
- Threading
- Tattooing
- Micro blading
- Tinting
- Makeup options, such as brow pencils, powders, gels and pomades

There are a few rules of symmetry when shaping the brow to frame your eye area.

Eyes, Ears and Brows

Step 1: To find where your eyebrow should start, imagine a vertical line running directly upwards from the indent of your nose. The point where it comes to rest on the inner section of the brow is where your eyebrow should start. You don't want to remove any hairs from the brow past this point.

Step 2: To find where the brow should end, imagine a diagonal line that runs from the outer edge of the base of your nostrils, past the outer edge of your eye. Any hairs outside that line can be removed.

Step 3: To find the highest point of your natural arch, imagine a vertical line that runs from the outer corner of your iris directly upwards to the eyebrow.

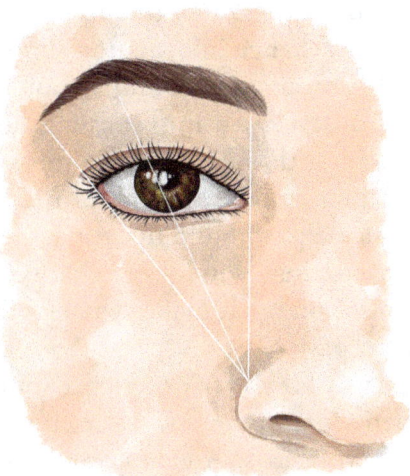

With these three guidelines, creating a shape becomes a lot easier. If you are trying to shape the brows with tweezers, stretch the area of skin you are tweezing from with one hand and with the other hand lay your tweezers as flat against the skin as possible. Remove the hair in the direction of the hair growth. This will help the hair lift more easily and painlessly.

If you are filling your brows with pencil, pomade or powder, make small hair-like strokes in the same direction as the brow hair. You only need to fill in any gaps you see in the brows. Blocked brows can look a little severe; replicating a natural look is generally more attractive. Once you've finished filling in the brows, having a clean spoolie (which looks like a clean mascara wand) on hand can help you blend what you've filled so that it looks more natural.

THE EARS

These small shell-shaped designs are miraculous in the way they enable us to take in our world through the vibrations of sound waves. Sound is the energy objects produce when they vibrate back and forth. Sound waves travel through the air, fluid or solid and transfer energy from the source of the sound, such as a bird chirping, to the space around it. Sound needs a source and a medium in order to travel. The air in the eardrum vibrates with a sound wave: the bigger the vibration, the louder the sound.

Humans have developed the use of this sound energy to create spoken language, enabling us to exchange information through words. Essentially, sound provides us with a means of communication.

Sound has also been developed into music. Music is a controlled use of sound vibrations coming through an instrument or voice and is also a system for communicating emotion. Think of the impact of background music in a movie. Music helps to build up suspense: the increase in tempo or a high pitch all work to draw you in. Alternatively, think about driving in your car and hearing a song that makes you feel free and alive or makes you reminisce about the past.

Your ears provide a way for you to experience sound; they also influence your ability to experience emotions. Ask yourself what messages have you been receiving through your ears? Are you open enough to truly hear the messages being delivered? Do you take the time to absorb what others have to say, or do you dismiss them too quickly to understand what they are all about? Do you need to listen to more uplifting music, or do you require more silence?

If you do take the time to hear others, not just with your ears but also with your whole being, you'll find the depth of your communication and connection with others will grow exponentially. Everybody likes to be heard. Everybody likes to feel understood. By being present when you listen to others you are acknowledging the gift that your ears provide. You're also more likely to hear the subtle nuances in their tone.

Sit for a moment now and return to the present. Stop whatever it is that you are doing and pay attention to the noises around you, whether it's a truck, an insect, an electrical gadget or a bird. Simply sit and hear everything you can. What a gift you have right here, right now to be able to hear the world around you. Rejoice in this gift.

Ears serve another function that you might have taken for granted: balance and hand–eye coordination. The inner ear controls our postural equilibrium and the body's orientation in space while travelling from one location to another. This happens in conjunction with other senses, such as vision. The reason that dancers are taught to focus on one spot when performing spins is in order to stop them from feeling dizzy. Similarly, when doing balancing postures in yoga you will be asked to keep your focus on one spot.

Try asking yourself: where am I going? Can I find a landmark? Where am I in relation to that spot? Now move! How could you apply this to your life in a broader context? Are there times where you feel as if everything around you is spinning? Could it be that a lack of focus on the things that matter is making everything feel unbalanced? Whenever you feel this lack of centre, ask yourself where you need to shift your focus. Let your inner compass be your guide.

Your ears are extremely delicate and need to be treated the same way you would treat any delicate items: with great care. Things like exercise, using ear plugs around loud noises, abstaining from using cotton buds in the ear canal, giving your ears a break from sound — especially after loud noises — every now and then, and keeping the volume down all contribute to long-term ear health.

Now that we know how vital our ears are and how to take care of them, let's turn to ways of embellishing them.

Earring styles

Earrings are a form of ornament hanging from or through the ears (principally the earlobes). They have been worn by both men and women throughout history.

The right set of earrings can highlight your face and your outfit. Firstly, find earrings that match your frame. Are you dainty and petite? Then massive hoops will overwhelm your face. If you're taller and wider-framed, a dainty drop style earring will get lost against the rest of your physique.

Secondly, find earrings made from materials that suit your sense of style. Gold and diamonds may be beautiful, but if you're into earthier, colourful styles and materials such as woods or semi-precious gemstones, flashy items won't match your wardrobe.

Thirdly, look for earring materials that suit your colouring. Earrings will draw attention to your face, particularly your eyes. Find earrings in a colour or tone that matches your eyes, hair and skin tone. Gold colours are great for people with warmer colouring, and silver tones are better for people with blue-based or cooler colouring (such as grey-blue eyes).

Finally, select an earring design that suits your face shape, hairstyle and the overall outfit you'll be wearing. If you can find shapes in your earrings that match the shapes found naturally in your eyes, jawline and chin, you'll find that the earrings harmonise better with your face. If you have a more rounded face shape or more rounded or curved elements to your face, then earrings with curved shapes will work better. If you have more angular lines in your face then geometric patterns will suit you when selecting earrings. You may have a combination of curves and angles, in which case leaf-style earrings, or earrings that incorporate both geometric and curved elements in their design will suit.

Below are a number of popular contemporary styles of earrings.

Dangle earrings

Dangle earrings are similar to drop earrings, as they fall below the earlobe. However, dangle earrings have more body and movement.

Jhumka

Jhumka are a traditional bell-shaped design from India. Indian brides often wear golden jhumka earrings.

Drop earrings

Drop earrings have a long, thin section that hangs from a stud-like back. May include a decorative end piece.

Teardrop

A teardrop is a drop earring with a teardrop shape.

Tassel

A tassel earring uses dangling threads of beads, gemstones, or actual cotton thread, held together by a central section. Known for its decorative edging effect, this style of earring is now quite popular as jewellery.

Chandelier

Chandelier earrings are another version of drop earrings, but they're longer, more complex and therefore more dramatic in their impact. This style falls near the jawline, making it great for framing the face.

Fringe-style earrings

Fringe-style earrings are mainly designed with a circular or oval plaque in the centre. A fringe has a fun bordering effect on jewellery. Current designs mix chains with small, varied cuts of diamonds, gemstones or beads to create a glittery effect.

Hoops

Hoops are round earrings that flow through the ears and connect at the other side. They come in a variety of sizes, metals and thicknesses.

Huggies

Huggies sit close to the earlobe or on the cartilage area of the ear. They sit more snugly than hoops, although they're still circular in shape.

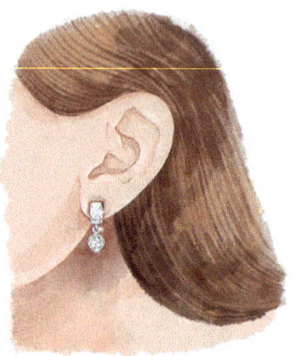 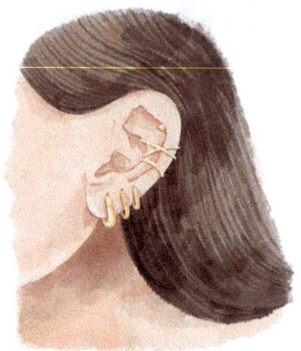

Studs

Studs are a basic, classic form of earring, comprising of a small piece of jewellery attached through the hole in the earlobe. The front section or stone sits on the lobe itself and is attached with a backing that locks the stud in place.

 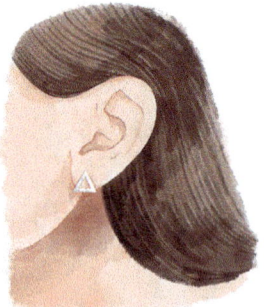

Cluster earrings

Cluster earrings are a decorative form of earrings, composed of gems, beads, glass or metal grouped together in a cluster. They're sometimes made of precious gems — such as the diamond-encrusted earrings regularly worn by brides — and are sometimes made of glass or plastic and worn as a disposable fashion item.

❦ Eyes, Ears and Brows ❧

 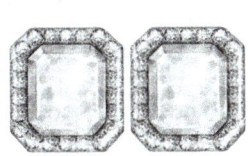 

Climbers

The climber style of earring sits in the ear in the same way as a stud; however, as its name implies, the shape of the earring climbs or curves up the ear from the lobe.

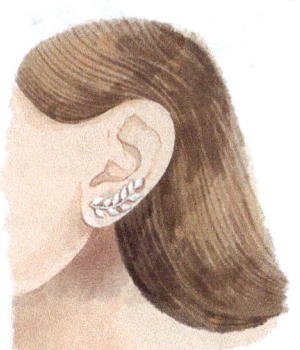 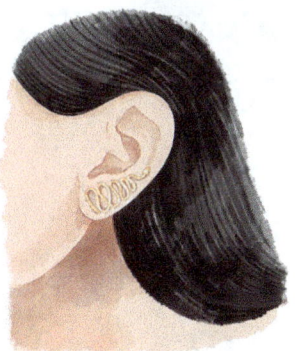

Best earring styles for different face shapes

When working out the best style of earring for your face shape, take a good look in the mirror. If you can, sweep your hair into a ponytail and examine your face. Look for the widest part. Is it your forehead, cheeks or jawline?

Then look at your jawline. Is it squarer, rounded or narrow? The reason for doing this exercise is to help you find your balancing out points. If you have a very angular chin and a wider forehead then finding an earring that has most of its weight near your jawline will help to add visual volume to this area, thereby balancing out and softening the overall look of the face.

Remember too that the closer you bring your earrings towards your eyes, the more you will bring the focus to them, as well as creating more of a youthful appearance. Conversely, the further your earrings drop, the more the more they will emphasize your face as a whole, drawing the eye to the jawline and lips for an alluring effect. Earrings that move also emphasise this area.

Your aim with earrings is to balance out any obvious gaps around your face or to emphasise the areas of your face that you like, such as your cheeks or your smile.

Face shapes chart

Round face shape

If your face is round, you will find that the widest point of your face is your cheeks. To balance out a round face, a dangling earring style looks great; search for earrings that have more weight at the base. Also look for curved elements in the earring design. If you have a shorter neck and a rounder face, make sure that your neckline is exposed if you want to wear extra-long, dangly earrings.

Round shape

Notice how the earrings (pictured above) are widest at the base. This allows the earrings to drop down and fill out underneath the cheek, near the jawline. This helps to balance out the roundness of the face.

Rectangular face shape

This is a narrow face shape in which the forehead, jaw and cheeks are similar widths. Here the aim is to add fullness around the cheek region. Create harmony by adding studs that are more rectangular in appearance, mimicking this face shape.

Dangly earrings can be worn, but aim to find earrings that have their widest section around the cheekbones, adding volume and giving the face more width.

Rectangle shape

Square-shaped face

Here the cheekbones and jawline are equal in width, and the width of the face is approximately equal to its length. Find geometric, square designs to mimic this natural shape. Straight edges and dangly earrings, such as squarer hoops, huggies or studs, will suit this face shape.

Square shape

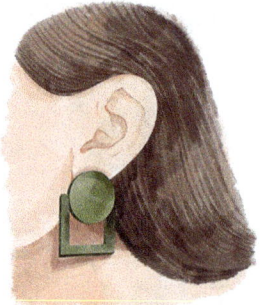

Oval face shape

Those blessed with this very symmetrical shape have forehead and cheeks of a similar width that gently taper down to the chin. Studs will draw attention to the center of the face. Hoops and teardrop styles also work well. This is a more versatile face shape so play away.

Oval shape

Eyes, Ears and Brows

Heart-shaped face

If your face is widest at the forehead and narrowest at the chin, you have a heart-shaped face. Balance out your face shape by placing emphasis on the jawline. Look for earrings that are slimmer at their attachment point (the ear lobe) and wider towards the base.

Dangle, teardrop and chandelier earrings work well to balance out this face shape.

Heart shape

Diamond face shape

This face shape has prominent cheekbones with a narrower forehead and chin. It is longer than it is wide. Look for dangly earrings that mimic yet soften the angles of your face. A dangling earring on a diamond face shape will create balance and harmony by adding volume to the jawline.

Great styles for this face shape include fringe, teardrop designs and chandelier style earrings.

Diamond shape

Chapter 15

Hair and Styling

HAIR

Moving up now to the crowning glory that is your hair. Your hair is the frame to your beautiful face. This is one part of us that allows for a great deal of creative expression. Get the cut or colour wrong, however, and you'll end up in hiding. I remember how devastated our golden retriever would be each summer when he was taken to the dog groomers for a haircut. He used to come home and hide under a tree all day. Genuine suffering occurred over those few lost inches of hair.

Multiply that suffering from a bad haircut by a thousand for a female human being. Unless you're living in a forest there's nowhere to run and hide. The top of the head is like the icing on a cake. It's the lid on a box. It's the peak. The summit. The end product. Something to aspire to. It's the closest part of the human anatomy to the sky, heavens or sun (whatever you want to worship).

That glorious mane of yours is sometimes displayed in its full brilliance — a 'good hair day' — or it can make you want to hit the fast forward button on the day if it doesn't behave itself: a 'bad hair' day.

When hair is manageable, the birds are singing, and life is fine. Your most attractive self steps into the limelight and you can tackle the world. If your hair looks great you look well-groomed.

When your hair is misbehaving, you look the opposite of well-groomed. Let's call it dishevelled. Unmanageable hair consists of frizzy bits and flyaways that dominate the surface of the head. Hair sits flat in places you don't want it to, and strands don't fall into place the way you need them to. A 'bad hair day' is not necessarily about what your hair looks like but about the impact it has on your self-esteem.

So why do we have hair on our heads anyway?

As a curly-haired girl, I used to believe that hair was there just to try my patience. However, now that I've finally embraced my curls, I see that hair can add character to the face.

A great haircut serves to frame the face, and a great colour works to enhance your skin's natural undertones and your eye colour. It even helps to brighten your smile. Well-styled hair, be it through the use of straightening, curling or styling products, definitely adds to a smart appearance.

From an evolutionary perspective, the hair on our head provides insulation and protection from the sun and its harmful UV rays. It also works to cool us down when we perspire, and the sweat evaporates from the hair.

Our hair allows us to express our identity and make a statement about who we believe we are and what our role in society is. A large part of our freedom, strength and power comes from here. So feel free to experiment with your hair. Thankfully it generally grows back!

Finding the right haircut/style to frame your face shape beautifully

Below is a breakdown of face shapes and hairstyles that help to balance them out.

Diamond face shape

The cheeks are the widest part of the face with this face shape, along with a more angular chin and narrower forehead. This shape looks great with hairstyles and cuts that add volume around the hairline or the jawline (or both). Pixie haircuts look great, as do bobs with layers at the front that angle in towards the face, adding volume to the jawline. Ensure that your haircut is at least chin length if choosing a longer option.

Styling tip: **add volume to the top of the head** (for example with a blow out) or add volume around the jawline by flicking the hair inwards.

❦ When Glamour Meets Gratitude ❦

Added volume at the top of the head balances out the forehead.

Middle part helps to open up the forehead.

Hair and Styling

Adding extra lift by styling the waves helps open out the forehead.

Oval face shape
With an oval face, you can pretty much wear any hairstyle you want, at any length.

Round Face shape

This face shape has a roundness at the forehead, cheeks and jawline, and will benefit from haircuts that visually break up the rounded shapes. Having layers in your hair is one way to create such an effect. Extra length will also make your face appear less round, as it draws attention down to the neck. Round face shapes should stick to hairstyles that are no shorter than the chin.

Styling tip: If you wear bangs, you will want to split them in the middle or to the side — another way to break up the roundness of the circular face shape. A centre parting can have a similar effect.

Side-swept fringe/bangs with lots of layers.

Side part with waves that are styled away from the face.

Side part with layers and hair flicked outwards.

Side part with layered waves.

Square face shape

This face shape is angular, with a forehead and jawline of similar width. If your concern is that your forehead is too wide, or you want to break up the symmetry of this face shape, then a side fringe will help. Another style that works well is the use of bangs that are shorter in the middle and then round out at the sides: this will make the face appear more oval-shaped.

If you feel that your jawline is too wide, use long hair to help elongate the face, softening the jawline and making it look more narrow. Ensure that the cut you opt for sits a little longer than the chin at the very least.

Styling tip: waves work to help to soften the angular edges of this face shape.

Waves soften a squarer jawline. The length of the hair takes away from the boxiness of the face shape.

All of these hairstyles (above) cut into the square shape of the face and break it up, using side parts, a full fringe or a sideswept fringe. Long waves provide extra softness, and curls around the jawline help to elongate the face shape.

Long face shape

This face shape is longer than it is wide, while cheeks, forehead and jawline are in similar proportions. To help balance this shape, it is best to opt for haircuts and styles that add volume around the cheeks, as this will add width to the face. Longer layers are a great option for this face shape, and it's best to keep the length of your hair below the chin.

Styling tip: if you choose to put waves through your hair, ensure that the face-framing waves kink at the cheekbones, adding width to your face. Alternatively, wearing a blunt set of bangs will reduce the length of the face.

Here we see style using volume through the centre of the face, which adds width to the overall face shape. Starting your curls at the cheekbones is a great way to gain this effect.

Notice how this straight bang cuts the face shape, making it appear less elongated.

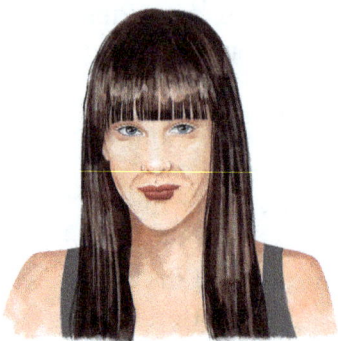 

Haircuts that fall just beneath the chin are also great for this face shape.

Heart face shape

This face shape has its greatest width at the forehead. A good way to balance it is to aim for haircuts and styles that take the width away from the forehead and move it to the jawline and chin. Hairstyles that sit at the chin line or a little below it also suit this face shape, as they bring more attention to the jawline.

Styling tip: side-swept fringes and side parts detract from the overall width of the forehead, especially if the wearer has a high forehead as well. Layers that curve into the face are another great styling option due to the volume they produce around the jawline.

Notice how the hair flicks inwards towards the jawline. This helps to add volume to this section of the face, giving attention to a very cute and angular chin.

Here we have a side parting that cuts across the forehead, with more volume at the base.

Side-swept fringes help to cut across a wider and more prominent forehead.

I hope this section has given you some new ideas about how to style your hair according to your face shape.

EXPRESSING GRATITUDE

Now that you've gained a clearer understanding of the symbolic nature of each body part, how it works, and what it allows you to experience, I invite you to take this knowledge and truly bless the body you stand in. The more gratitude and love you are able to demonstrate towards your body, the better it will perform.

If you keep being told 'You're not good enough' you will end up believing it, especially if it's what you keep telling yourself . Even if you're creating amazing things, you may not see how amazing they are, due to this belief. Imagine the messages that would become stored in your body if, on a daily basis, you continued to repeat horrible phrases like 'You're not tall enough, skinny enough, sexy enough, funny enough, pretty enough, perfect enough'.

Let's imagine, for example, that you are trying to lose weight. If you keep telling yourself you're too fat, you will sabotage any healthy weight loss, because the subconscious mind has a way of acting out your belief systems and putting you in situations that reinforce your beliefs. It's like having an awful boss who never gives you praise and only offers criticism: instead of performing at your best you'll operate from fear, always worrying that whatever you produce won't be good enough. You'll never satisfy. Contrast this with a boss who says, 'Wow. I love what you're doing here. Can I have more of that? Great work.' All of a sudden, you're working from a place of love, joy and potential. You move forward with a greater level of confidence, knowing that even if you make a mistake it won't be the end of the world, just part of a learning curve.

IT'S THE SAME WITH YOUR BODY!!!!

If you give your body words of criticism, judgement and harshness, a protective barrier will start to form. Negative self-talk creates a fear-based frequency in the body that translates into many unwanted and unconscious ailments. You might experience excess weight, a fearful and defensive heart, lungs that only breath a shallow breath, restricted movement, tightness in the neck and shoulders, digestive difficulties or trouble sleeping.

Instead, give yourself praise and encouragement. Tap into how you would prefer to feel and feel those feelings. Suddenly you're giving yourself the freedom to let go of all of those barriers to self-love. A perfect body, height or weight is not actually what you are after. You were always perfect. It's only through comparison that you suddenly become 'imperfect'.

Marketing campaigns do a brilliant job of feeding us the story that we are not as perfect as the fourteen to sixteen-year-old with a flat stomach, airbrushed hips and buttocks, and a photogenic grin, oozing sex appeal. I've been on enough photo shoots as a hair and makeup artist to know the level of production that goes into creating that one image. A whole team is involved, including a photographer, hair stylist, makeup artist, set designer, clothing stylist and retoucher. The model walks in with dark circles, pimples and flat hair, and the styling team goes to work to achieve perhaps a 'no-makeup look', or a look that says 'I've just rolled out of bed'. However, that look will take two hours to attain. The stylists make sure that the highest-end garments are worn. The model twists and turns, knowing all of her best angles and lines. She does a pretend laugh and a head flick, so that it looks to the camera as if she's having a great time, when really she's still hung over from the night before, or just wants to get back home to her boyfriend or read a book.

The photographer gauges the best lighting and composition for his model and directs her accordingly. Hair and makeup are constantly running back on set to do touch-ups. Six to eight hours later the shoot is finalised. Now the editing and retouching begins.

Out of the hundreds of photos taken during the day there will be a handful selected as worthy for retouching. Let's see, hmmm. Cellulite? No, the model doesn't have any of that because it isn't socially appealing. It's gone with one swipe of a blending tool in editing software. Nor does the model have any breakouts. The makeup artist has worked hard to cover them because they aren't socially desirable. Nor are under-eye bags. The retoucher can also use a blending tool to eliminate any of these offensive features.

I hope I'm getting my point across here. Sometimes we are presented with unachievable goals. Yes, the picture looks lovely. Yes, it would be lovely to go back to having porcelain teenaged skin. But if that's what you really want, the process described above is what will be required of you each and every day.

If we buy the marketer's product, we are guaranteed the hope of achieving youth, desirability, confidence, lifestyle and validation from others. Just a little irony on my part! All of those attributes actually come from within, not from without in the form of clothing, product or lifestyle.

Marketers are telling you that you 'aren't there yet', that you 'haven't arrived' but that if you purchase their product you'll experience the feeling you're after. In other words they've created an image for you that transports you into some potential future. All you have to do is purchase their product and your life will be complete.

I'm not saying that you shouldn't bother trying to improve on what you've got. Otherwise this book would have been a complete waste of time. It's essential to take pride in your appearance and capitalise on your assets. It's almost a way of paying homage to yourself. My only issue is when I see women dress to be the version of somebody else that they aspire to be, rather than dressing for who they actually are. In doing so they often overlook the assets they have.

I've seen countless social media videos where the person receiving the makeover is gorgeous; however, they are given a makeover that makes them look like the most popular Hollywood star of the time and their natural beauty becomes masked. In an attempt to look like somebody else, they end up ignoring the most important person in the room: themselves. Stop comparing yourself to an illusion. The aim of this book was to encourage you to dress in line with the person that you actually are. To express your own inner style. Why shouldn't you have the same feelings and experiences that marketers are offering you, but on your own? You have the power of imagination. You can create a vision of how you would like your life to be in your mind. And you can sit in that feeling and experience a sexier version of yourself, a healthier, more confident and social version of yourself.

Try it! If you need to, create a vision board first. If not, just close your eyes and see the version of yourself that you would prefer to see.

What are you doing, how are you behaving? What are your experiences? Who is around you, what are they saying to you? What actions did you take on a regular basis to become this version of yourself? How is it different from the person standing in front of the mirror today?

Nothing external has the capacity to provide a desired internal feeling. It has to come from within. You may feel a slight improvement on first purchasing your shiny new item from the marketers. You may even feel as if you're part of an elite club, depending on the price you paid, but this feeling will fade. What you really want is to have confidence, pride in your appearance, increased energy and vitality, self-love and validation from others. If that's the case, practise having those feelings daily. Especially when you're having a bad hair day. Practice feeling sexy, confident and proud, practice feeling vital and energetic, practice the feeling of self-love. This is the way to foster these emotions, rather than through the continual purchase of marketed products.

Gratitude exercise

Pay attention to the way that you currently feel about your body and physical appearance. Write the feelings down, without suppressing or dismissing any of them. I want you to genuinely acknowledge where you're at with yourself, because how you feel about yourself right now will translate into your future physical reality.

Once you've been brutally honest about how you feel, I then want you to get in touch with how you would prefer to feel about yourself. Play with those feelings of confidence, sexiness and so forth. Acknowledge the positive feelings without judgement, just as we did with the negative feelings. If you feel resistance, remind yourself that this is an exercise in play and imagination. Imagination is by far the most powerful and underused resource in our toolkit. Imagination can override multiple inbuilt systems. Imagination got us to the moon and back. Tell your resistant voice — 'Hey, I'm just imagining. Get off my back please and let me focus on these feelings for the next five minutes'.

When you were a child all you did was play, all day every day. As adults, most of us have lost that sense of play and wonder. This is the time to play make believe and envision a different role, a different reality for yourself. Have as much fun with this as you possibly can.

Keep playing, and watch all of the excess baggage and physical ailments start to drop away, allowing you to move forward with ease, energy, vibrancy and authenticity. Kinder words of encouragement to yourself will kick in, overriding the harsh and judgmental ones.

There is an affirmation that I love to use, but don't force it on yourself if you're not ready for it. The affirmation is: 'I am perfect, whole and complete'. Try it on for size. See how it feels. Is there resistance? How much? Do you think you can grow into that affirmation? Not yet? That's fine.

Ask yourself instead: How would it feel to be perfect, whole and complete? Let that thought linger. You could repeat it a few times when you're in the shower, starting a new job, or going on a new date. Aim towards embodying the affirmation 'I am perfect, whole and complete' by beginning with baby steps. Keep asking yourself how it would feel, until you're ready to wear the 'perfect, whole and complete' outfit with confidence and pride.

From this place we can move forward and begin to express the beauty that lies within.

Chapter 16

Becoming Resourceful

> 'Becoming resourceful through gratitude is the only way to truly recognise what you've got.'

MINE YOUR INNER RESOURCES

By now you've learned just how amazing your body is. You're aware of how your body works. You've discovered some self-care options to help honour and appreciate your body, as well as ways to enhance each area. It's time to make use of this knowledge.

Anyone who is successful in life has looked within and asked: What do I have? What are my resources? How can I make the most of them? How can I best utilise what I have within and around me? What are my strengths, skillsets and natural abilities? What do I love?

If they didn't value their resources and give their time to practising things they love to do, they wouldn't be able to realise their full potential. And as economic and dry as this may seem, your body is a resource, an asset.

You have a miraculous body that serves you daily. It will serve you for the rest of your life if you honour it and treat it with respect. Show your body some appreciation, rather than the criticism and harshness it is so used to receiving.

That harsh, critical voice is driven by fear and insufficiency. It compares itself to others and feels it needs to compete with them for love and acceptance. Yet there is plenty of love to go around, so ditch the scarcity mentality and keep a sharp eye out for fear-based thoughts.

Fear, often fear of rejection, is an emotion that blocks love, and blocks your ability to see how beautiful you truly are. It keeps you distracted. Don't let fear rule your thoughts. Come back to a place of loving appreciation instead and very soon you'll gain a new perspective on yourself.

It is often said that your outer world is a reflection of your inner world. Living from a place of inadequacy and comparison won't bring you success. Acknowledging and appreciating what you have is the first stage of resourcefulness. Once you reach this state you'll be able to appreciate your worth and get the most out of everything you do have to offer.

If you've ever had the experience of a full closet but nothing to wear, you're probably in the category of not appreciating what you have. It's not that you have nothing to wear, it's just that you haven't taken the time to really assess what you have and how you can make the most of it.

During my teenage years in high school, I had a friend who was always immaculate. Her shoes were polished, her clothes were freshly pressed, her school bag was always neat and tidy. Her school textbooks were in mint condition and her pencil case was clean. Every item she owned was taken care of.

◅❦ Becoming Resourceful ❦▻

Interestingly, she had fewer items of clothing, shoes and stationery than most; but whatever she had was taken care of with the utmost attention. This is something I've noticed about people who are grateful: they care for what they do have and as a consequence, what they have is quality.

Instead of purchasing items of clothing with a consumer mentality, they look at their wardrobe as an investment. They take time to find the piece that fits exactly with what they want. They pay careful attention to the details of their items: the fit, the material, the stitching. When they obtain what they want they take good care of it. They maintain their resources. They read the care instructions. They ensure that the area where they store or leave their item is clean and tidy.

As a consequence, they end up surrounded by items that give them constant joy, clothes that they are proud to wear and own. Their items last longer, fit better and look great for years. In taking this level of pride and care with whatever they have, they end up needing far less. At the end of the day, gratitude and respect for what you have is more satisfying than continually acquiring more.

BECOMING RESOURCEFUL IN YOUR WARDROBE

To become more resourceful about your wardrobe, start thinking about quality over quantity. Consider your clothes and accessories as assets: this will assist you to begin the process of shopping *inside your wardrobe.*

Every journey needs to begin from within — looking outwards for your answers leads to distraction and confusion.

This exercise will require you to acknowledge what you actually need, based on what you already have. Your wardrobe will look better on you if you take into consideration whether you have a cooler or a warmer skin tone. Within a wardrobe of mostly cool or mostly warm colours, blending your wardrobe will be a much more seamless process. A dash of colour in an alternate tone can look interesting, for example when accessorising. However, a cool-coloured top generally won't go with a warm-coloured skirt or pants.

Once you know whether you are best suited to cool or warm colours, it is easy to get mileage from your wardrobe. With a creative use of different tops, jackets, and accessories (bags, scarves, shoes, belts and jewellery) the same pair of pants or skirts can be remixed over and over again. A quality pair of warmer (sand, beige, camel, mustard, olive or tan) or cooler (bone, mushroom, navy, charcoal, black, cool grey) coloured smart casual pants can be dressed up or down to fit either a semi-formal or casual occasion. A dressy top could be used over two separate skirts, like a business skirt and a going out skirt, or over jeans if that's your preference.

Using your wardrobe as your first shopping destination allows you to identify clothing gaps and thereby gives you a more focused and practical approach to purchasing new clothes.

Think of creating *outfits* rather than looking for pieces or items. This is the difference between someone with great style and someone who occasionally gets it right. Always try to think of three different ways you could wear an item of clothing. Think about how you can wear the same garment so that it's more formal, as well as dressed down in such a way that you could go and meet a friend for coffee. Consider how you might use particular accessories at home to transform a shirt or dress.

Next time you go to buy a shirt, don't purchase it unless you can think of at least three different ways you could wear it. Is it a warm or a cool colour? Does it go with any of the skirts, jeans or pants that you currently have?

If not, unless you purchase a whole new ensemble, it will just sit in your wardrobe gathering dust.

Resourcefulness is a quality that you need to activate in all areas of your life. When you create a wardrobe, you are investing in the way you present yourself to others. Your wardrobe is an advertisement for your inner self.

The exercise of really scrutinising what you have in your wardrobe and utilising it to its greatest potential will have a knock-on effect in other areas of your life.

> 'Whatever you appreciate … appreciates.' Lynne Twist, author of *The Soul of Money*

However, you won't be able to truly see what you have if you have too much 'stuff' in your wardrobe that is never worn. Perhaps it is too tight or in the wrong colour, has prints or patterns that are off, is in an outdated style, needs mending, or was just a really bad choice at the time but was so expensive that you don't want to throw it away.

Holding onto clothes you don't wear limits your ability to strengthen your resourcefulness muscle. It's the equivalent of keeping ingredients you dislike in your fridge and pantry. Instead of throwing them out, you tell yourself you can't let them go because you spent too much money on them, or that one day you'll buy all of the sister ingredients to cook that exotic dish.

My point is, only keep clothes in your closet that you can and will use. If you don't, won't or can't wear them you'll never have anything to wear! You cannot maximise your assets when you stuff your closet full of unworkable resources.

Start by creating an inventory of your closet. Become aware of what you actually have in your wardrobe before you tell yourself that you 'simply have nothing to wear'.

YOUR WARDROBE INVENTORY

Step 1: Remove what you never wear

Your closet has a limited amount of space. Think of each item of clothing as taking up valuable real estate in your closet. You don't have to throw anything away just yet unless you want to. The key here is to acknowledge what doesn't get worn anymore and ask the following questions.

What needs to be discarded because it's showing strong signs of wear and tear?

This is the easiest section to cull so start here. Pull the items out of your closet and place them in the 'out' pile. However, the fact that they were worn so much means that something about the item really worked for you. Work out what it was that you loved about this item before completely letting go of it. Was it the neckline? The colour? The cut? The texture? The hem length? Knowing this will make it easier to replace the item. It may also be that this style or colour of item harmonises really well with the rest of your wardrobe.

What items don't you like anymore?

Pull them out of your closet and place in the out pile. Before you give it the official farewell, ask yourself why you didn't like the item. Was it ill fitting? If so, where on your body didn't it fit? Did it make you feel fat or frumpy? Was it that no matter what you tried to wear it with it just didn't work? Was it too shapeless? Was it a colour that made you feel grey or washed out each time you put it on? Was it too loud for your personality? Or too risqué? Was it too boring? Did it make you feel self-conscious?

At this stage of your wardrobe audit, assess your past choices. Some were made on impulse, some unconsciously. Train yourself to recognise your unwise choices so that you don't make the same mistake. The more you do this, the better you will become at making smarter, more considered choices that suit your needs, wants and lifestyle.

What doesn't fit?

Are any of your clothes too loose, too long or too boxy? Pull them out of your closet and work out whether they can be altered to fit. Are you willing to invest in alterations to make these items work? If yes, then place them in the alterations pile. Put the rest into an out pile or a 'can't make up my mind' pile. If the items are too tight you generally can't alter them. You'll need to ask yourself whether you're willing to do what it takes to fit into this item of clothing. If so, by when? Put it into a container and store it in the 'to be reviewed in 6 to 12 months' pile. Mark the date on your calendar so that you actually review the garment when you say you will. But get it out of your wardrobe so that you have one less reason to stop beating yourself up or feeling depressed about your current weight or shape.

What just doesn't look right?

Maybe you spent an absolute fortune on this item, so you're finding it really hard to let go. Maybe it's not a style that works for you anymore. You've outgrown your grunge look and you're not sure that trend will work its way back. If you can't bring yourself to pop this item in the out pile then place it in the 'can't make up my mind' pile.

What do you promise yourself you will wear one day but never do?
If you haven't worn a particular item for a long time, you may need to alter the item (alterations pile), let it go (out pile) or make a decision about it later ('can't make up my mind' pile). Alternatively, the item might not fit your lifestyle. In this case, it would need to go into a non-lifestyle fitting pile.

This pile is for items that may look great on you but that you no longer have an occasion to wear: for example, a business suit for an at-home mum. That's fine, life evolves and so does your closet. You don't have to get rid of the outfit if you feel it still resonates, but it doesn't need to take up valuable space in your wardrobe. Consider treating the non-lifestyle fitting pile the same way you would your winter and summer wardrobe. Generally, you'll store away your winter clothes in summer and vice versa, so that you can see what is actually available for use in your closet. You can treat your non-lifestyle fitting pile in a similar way, especially if the items in this pile look good on you when worn.

You can also treat your 'can't make up my mind' pile this way. Grab a storage container and label it. Then move it out of your closet so that it's not visible each time you look on your hangers. If you are drawn to a massive gap in your wardrobe because the item is no longer available, you can always let it back into your closet later on. But for now, you want to work with the parts of your wardrobe that are fitting and functional.

The 'can't make up my mind' pile will be part of your second wardrobe review. Anything that goes into this pile *must* be tried on. The garment may look better or worse than you thought it did. You may need to come back to this pile on another day if you're feeling too overwhelmed or tired. You need to be in the right headspace to do a wardrobe audit properly, so don't feel that you have to complete all parts of your wardrobe audit in one sitting. Wardrobe audits are ongoing. Your body, personal preferences and lifestyle requirements evolve and so should your wardrobe.

As for the out pile, that's pretty self-explanatory. Throw the items away, give them to your local charity shop or sell them on consignment.

◈─ Becoming Resourceful ─◈

Finally, we come to the alterations pile. Alterations are something that should be factored into the majority of purchases. It's rare to find perfectly fitting outfits straight off the rack, unless you're blessed with a standard body type.

See Chapter 17 for greater detail on alterations and how they can improve your outfit. When your garments fit you like a glove, you will automatically appear slimmer and more stylish.

After this cleanse, only items that enhance you, maximize your attributes and make you feel good about yourself will remain in your wardrobe.

It's also possible to expand this concept into the rest of your life. Where else can you eliminate, avoid or limit situations and people that bring you down? As your wardrobe comes down in size and your life becomes less overloaded, you will start feeling better about yourself in general, knowing that everything you have around you is serving you well.

Your wardrobe is not only an investment: it also reflects your inner world. Start believing in your beautiful inner and outer world and discard the offensive pile you never wear anyway. It wants to go — there are other bodies these items could be serving better.

By freeing up space in your wardrobe, you are freeing up space for a newer, fresher look to enter. Each item that enters your wardrobe is taking up valuable real estate (in your closet), in addition to money and effort, as you need to look after, wash, iron and store each item you purchase. The more consciously each item is chosen, the more your wardrobe will become a true reflection of who you currently are.

A less cluttered wardrobe also means you can see what you're working with. And you'll have the magnificent wardrobe quality that makes my heart sing: *order*! The more order I see, the more I know that someone has a grip on things in that area of their life. Make that area your wardrobe.

Step 2: What style do you want to reflect?

One of the most important questions you can ever ask yourself in life is 'What do I want?' Too often we focus on what we don't want, what we don't like. It's really easy to do this. It's our brain's default mode to notice what is wrong about things. Being clear instead about what you want will catapult you forward in life. It's totally worth the effort and energy. And when it comes to your wardrobe you will never be inspired by your closet if you don't have an understanding of what you want when it comes to style.

Do the items in your wardrobe make you smile each time you look at them? Do they reflect the person you are, or the qualities of the person you want to become? Do you feel amazing each time you try a particular item on?

When you think of style, what do you think of? Everybody has a different perspective on style and what it means. This is why we all have different tastes, even when something is dictated as 'trendy' by the fashion industry. At the end of the day it's not what the major fashion houses offer us each season that matters it's what we select.

Now that you have a wardrobe of clothes that you actually wear, take a close look at what's inside. Are the clothes making you feel excited? Or are you a little bored with what you see? Functionality is a great thing, but sometimes you need to shake things up a bit. This could be through the addition of a newer piece or accessory, or wearing something that you've had for a long time in a different way. Same same, but different. And that's fashion in general. You don't have to eliminate everything and start all over again if you're bored. You just need to try coming from a fresh perspective.

What have you got that you do wear?

There will always be favourite items that you wear on a regular basis. You receive compliments when you wear the item, it's practical, it fits you comfortably. It makes you look and feel good and has given your purse a great return on investment (cost per wear). These trusty faithfuls are the items that matter most when you want to consider developing your wardrobe. How do you feel when you wear them? Work out what you like about each of them. Is it the colour, the design, the way it fits, the fabric or the neckline? Do any of these items need replacing? If so, these are clothes that you can invest a little more money in (for a quality cut and material) because you know they work for you.

How many ways can you wear the items in your closet?

Now it's time to play! Grab a top or pair of pants and see how many ways you can wear it. A basic t-shirt can be dressed up or down according to the pants or skirt you add to it. Accessories — shoes (heels, flats or sneakers), scarves, jewellery, handbags, belts — and extra layers (jackets, cardigans, blazers etc.) can give your boring t-shirt a new lease of life. You may have worn that t-shirt as part of a single go-to outfit and never explored any further. Keep exploring and playing. Go through your wardrobe one piece at a time. It will make you see possibilities that you never knew existed. Take photos of yourself in different outfits so you can remember what worked.

As you go through this process you'll also notice that there are certain items that could make a great outfit if you had a different pair of pants — extra layers such as blazers or jackets, or a different style of shoes to go with them. Or you might notice, for example that you have daytime handbags but not enough small clutches for going out at night.

When Glamour Meets Gratitude

Work out your lifestyle requirements

How much time do you spend exercising? How many hours are you at home or at work? Is work more corporate or casual? How often do you attend formal events and smart casual events? How much of a party animal are you? Are you in a warm or cool climate most of the time? Your lifestyle may have changed when you changed jobs, for example from a corporate environment to work that requires a uniform. You may then find that the majority of your wardrobe is in need of an update. Are there ways to dress down your corporate garments before you push them into the donation pile?

If there is a lifestyle imbalance in your wardrobe (relative to the number of hours you spend in certain activities in your day), you'll find yourself not being able to get the most out of your wardrobe, even though you may have plenty of clothes.

Make a plan based on what inspires you

Before you hit the shops it's always great to have a plan. There's no better plan than one based on inspiration. If you see looks that you would love to try, pay attention to them. Google and Pinterest are amazing sources of inspiration. Many celebrities have stylists so their outfits are often thrown together beautifully. If you have an idea of your body shape you can google celebrities with that shape and take a look at the outfits they tend to wear. This will help you select better designs for yourself.

Let's say, for example, that you're inspired by an outfit including a graphic t-shirt with a silver pleated skirt, white trainers and a leather jacket. In your wardrobe you find a grey skirt and a black blazer and a graphic t-shirt that matches. However, you don't have white trainers. And although you might have black or silver heels, you would like to add a funky street style to your outfits, which you feel you could obtain from a pair of white or silver trainers. Could this be something that would upgrade and enhance your outfit options? What other outfits could your white or silver trainers go with if you were to invest in them? Would their addition give a completely new vibe to your current wardrobe?

As you can see, you don't need to buy an entire new wardrobe, just a few additional items that give you more options in how you put together your current wardrobe. An update, so to speak.

Create a vision board of outfits that you love. It could also include patterns, colours, textures, and accessories. Copy and paste these into a word document or online pin board or, if you're old school, onto a piece of cardboard. You'll start noticing a theme. It may be flares, a textured pullover, a ruffled skirt or a bold pop of colour. This will be a guide to what you need to try on when you're shopping, as it excites your senses and being excited by your wardrobe is key.

Shop with the aim of developing *outfits* for your wardrobe, not one-off items that don't tie in with what you already have.

ALWAYS HAVE SOMETHING TO WEAR BY CREATING A CLOTHING CAPSULE

The idea of the clothing capsule was conceived by Susie Faux back in the 1970s. It consists of essential clothing items, such as skirts and trousers (outfit bottoms); blouses, shirts, knits, sweaters (outfit tops); and coats, jackets, blazers, cardigans (outwear) that never go out of fashion. These can then be matched with seasonal and trendy pieces.

The purpose of a clothing capsule is to keep the number of clothes you have in your wardrobe to a minimum, while obtaining maximum wear from each individual item. You can organise your clothing capsule into different clothing modules, such as seasonal modules, or formal/casual/active-wear modules. If you're lucky, your lifestyle may allow you to mix different clothing modules to gain maximum versatility from your capsule wardrobe. If your work attire is smart casual, it's easy to mix items from your work-clothing module with your going-out clothing module or your basics/essentials clothing module, especially if they follow a colour scheme that ties in with other modules.

What exactly is a clothing module?

A clothing module is a complete group of garments that mix and match with each other harmoniously. Start by choosing a colour palette to base your module on. The way to work this out is to find tops, skirts or pants with the most colour options present. Some women like to wear more colour on their lower half and others prefer it in their tops. And some reject colour point blank, protesting 'I only ever wear neutrals!' Whatever your preference may be, find your most colourful items, or most popular neutrals, and build your modules around these.

You can then create a lifestyle (work, lounge wear, or active-wear) module. This will consist of three or four blouses, shirts, or t-shirts (outfit tops) and at least one skirt or pair of pants/jeans (outfit bottoms). The top-to-bottom ratio should be roughly 2:1. Add at least one piece of outer wear such as a jacket, blazer, coat or cardigan. There is no better way to gain maximum wear from a garment than with the use of accessories, so have a couple of accessory options for each module.

In total, clothing modules contain 6–10 items of clothing. When it's done effectively, you can easily create 6–18 outfits from a single module. Combined with other matching clothing modules, your outfit choices should see you through most of the year. Just make sure you catalogue each outfit with a picture so that you remember your options. This will make early morning dressing a lot simpler. Once you have taken the time to organise your clothing capsule, based on your different lifestyle modules, you'll never look back.

The reason clothing modules work so well is because they allow you to become very clear about how you wish to present yourself. The process forces you to sit down and develop a wardrobe strategy that identifies garments suitable to the version of yourself you wish to embody, piece by piece. This is a strategic and budget-friendly way of dealing with your wardrobe, since the result is more wear per item. This does not mean cheap. On the contrary, having less to buy means that you can invest in higher quality items and gain maximum value from each.

It also lessens the burden of moving into a new style direction and takes the headache out of getting ready each morning.

If you're in a style rut — are bored with your current wardrobe, or don't feel that your clothes work very well together and want to move into a fresher, more aligned style — then the use of a clothing module is a great place to start. When you have base outfits to work from, it becomes easy to identify the gaps in your wardrobe, based on completing an outfit, rather than focusing on individual pieces.

I hope that by this stage you've realised that having an effective wardrobe isn't about the number of items you possess. It's about maximising the wear of each item and coordinating it with the other items in your capsule.

I can't wait for you to discover the endless potential you can create with a workable wardrobe! It's full of quality garments that you love wearing, that suit you, give you versatility and flatter your figure.

Chapter 17

On Fitting In and Measuring Up

FITTING IN

Brenee Brown tells us that 'true belonging only happens when we present our authentic and true selves to the world' and that 'fitting in emerges as the primary barrier to belonging'. In other words, the more we try to gain other people's approval and fit their mould, or society's mould, the less we will feel as though we truly belong.

How can another value and love who you are if you don't express the real you? Telling another person what they want to hear, or behaving in a certain way, may gain a nod of approval and draw less criticism from the other person. However, it doesn't facilitate more than a one-way relationship. They're clear on what's working for them and they assume that you're always in agreement. Why fix something that doesn't need mending? The other person won't find out what it is that you really need, want and desire, and they'll never see what lights you up from the inside. Instead, you'll simply become one of their followers.

But when they fall in love with someone, they will tolerate opposition to their point of view, they will respect how imperfect that person can be. What's different about this person that they cherish and adore from you, who always toed the line and did as you were supposed to do? The other person showed up with a greater sense of *self*-approval. They didn't need it from outside. Fitting in is never the answer. Yet so many of us do it, both in our personal lives and in the way we express ourselves stylistically.

On Fitting In and Measuring Up

This idea of fitting in, measuring up, being perfect and making another person happy (at our own expense) has been a female social construct for far too long. It leads to unhealthy behaviour: crash dieting in order to fit a particular size of clothing or wearing shoes that cut off the circulation.

When an item of clothing hugs the wrong spot, making you try and cover your tummy or tug at it to move it into place, then it doesn't fit. You need to alter the outfit so that it does fit, or find an alternative item. I see so many women wearing ill-fitting items because the design is trendy, or going to a night club wearing skirts, pants or backless tops that they are spilling out of. It's not sexy! It looks uncomfortable and it screams 'trying too hard'!

It's like a bad relationship where one person wants the other so much that they try to change who they are in order to be with the other person. It ends up being uncomfortable and awkward for both parties, and it never works. You'll eventually find your perfect partner when you accept yourself. Do the same with your body and your wardrobe will flatter you, not frustrate you.

> "Celebrate the form and the fit will be just perfect." **J.Stepanik**

When you find a relationship or friendship that's compatible, it brings out the best in you. It's the same with clothes. Wear clothes that fit you properly and you're three quarters of the way to becoming the style queen that you were born to be.

MEASURING UP

We're perfect until we begin comparing ourselves to others, when we focus outside ourselves and suddenly we're not enough. Not tall enough, not skinny enough, not pretty enough: the list is never-ending. Instead of focusing on our own attributes we see only what we are lacking in comparison to that other person.

Let's reverse that now and pay attention to your favourite features. Scan every area of your body. Note down what you like about yourself and why. This could be a completely foreign exercise to many, but I'm asking you to pay attention to what makes you unique and attractive. This will enable you to highlight your assets and your strengths. If you don't appreciate your assets, they won't grow roots and flourish. You therefore need to start shining some light onto how valuable and beautiful you truly are.

When you are truly grateful for the way you look, the body you've been given, the curves, the height and weight, the size of your nose, the colour and shape of your eyes, mouth and hair; then you can truly transform the way you look and feel.

You can stand in front of the mirror, see your beauty and recognise that you are enough: good enough, pretty enough, tall enough, skinny enough. You're enough! You always have been. When you can do this, or when you have the courage to try (as uncomfortable a process as this may be), your journey of inner transformation will begin.

To bring this knowledge into the area of fashion and presentation, start with a tape measure. Measure yourself. You'll love the difference it makes to your shopping adventures, and the ease it provides in selecting outfits. It astonishes me how many people shop for clothes without knowing their measurements. Then they arrive home and realise that the item doesn't sit quite right. The quick use of a measuring tape would have forestalled this dilemma and the need to go back and exchange the item.

You won't be able to truly enhance your physical attributes when they're in ill-fitting attire. Not obtaining proper body measurements can lead to trying on clothing that is too small and seeing lumps and bumps in all the wrong places, prompting negative self-talk: 'I'm getting fat. I look awful. Nothing fits me!' This leads to: 'Bah. I don't want to try on any more clothes, this is no fun.' Making a measuring tape your next investment will solve this situation before it arises. Pretty much all online shopping sites have sizing charts.

I will add that there is virtually no consistency left in clothing sizes. You will need to reference each clothing house's sizing charts to work out where you fit.

Important measurements to know:

1. *The fullest part of your bust*: you can find this measurement by bringing the tape under your arms and around to the fullest part

☙ On Fitting In and Measuring Up ☙

of your bust. It's best to do this with your bra on, ensuring that the tape sits flush against your back and is parallel to the ground. This is an especially useful measurement to know if you have a larger bust, as you'll often find that shirts don't sit comfortably around the bust area. Knowing this measurement will help you work out whether you need to go up a size in the top you are after and bring in the side seams for a better fit, or whether you need to look at other options.

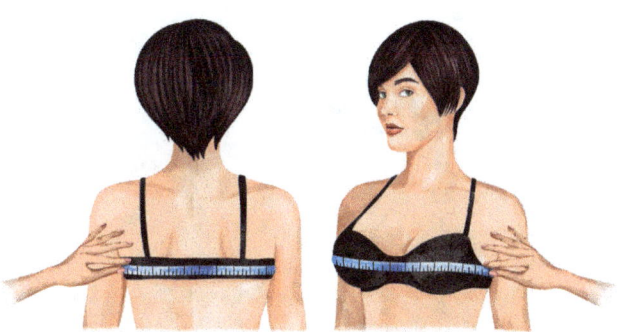

2. Your *natural waist or the smallest part of your torso*. You can often find this measurement by bending sideways. The part of your body that indents is your natural waist. If you have a smaller waist than the standard clothing make, it's best to make alterations for this section part of your budget.

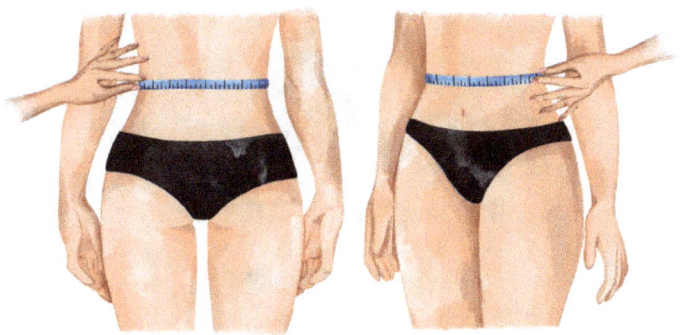

3. *Your hips.* This measurement is found most easily by taking a look at your butt and working out its widest part. Stand with your feet together and from the widest part of your seat (backside) draw an imaginary line around the hips. Getting this measurement right will stop you from getting the horizontal lines around the leg crease that occurs when pants are too tight around the butt.

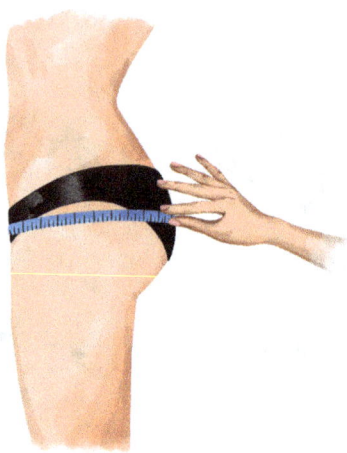

4. *Shoulder line.* This is an important measurement, as it will enable you to identify if a shirt or blouse will fit you properly across the shoulders. (You will have more freedom of movement in the arms if it fits properly.) This measurement is found by placing your measuring tape across the back and measuring from one shoulder to the other.

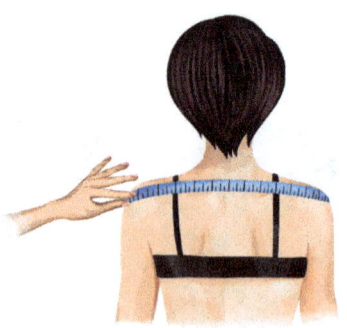

5. *Inseam.* This starts at your crotch and ends at the bottom of your leg. It determines the size of inseam you should opt for (tall, petite or regular).

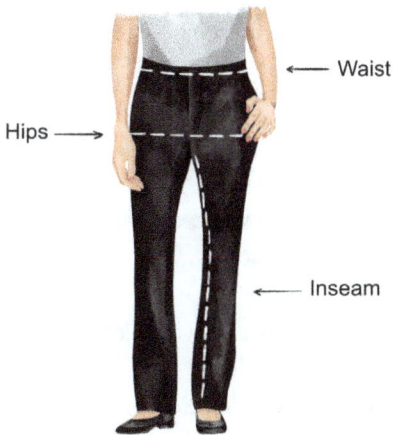

Let's say you don't have your measuring tape with you, and you're trying on a few items of clothing at the shops. You might be questioning whether you can get away with a little bit of tugging fabric in the wider or more rounded areas of your body, because you feel that going up a size will make the garment too big. Any pinching or gathering, where fabric is seen to pull, means the item is too small. Don't buy it! A garment will always look best when it sits flat against your body, not clinging, bunching or pulling. Go up a size and make alterations to the garment if you feel you have to have this particular piece. If you see any of the following, you know that you need to look for a larger size that you can alter to fit:

- Too tight in the underarm area. If the arm holes are cut too small, you will never be able to alter this and won't be able to move properly in the shirt.

- Buttons tugging or popping open at the bust. If you can't pull your arms down and behind you when you have the top or jacket on, your bust doesn't have enough space and you will constantly be having problems with gaping buttons. Save yourself the embarrassment and headache. Try a larger size or move on.

- If the sleeves are passing your wrist and covering your hands, the item will definitely need altering.

- If pants are too long at the ankles or skirts are too long for your stature, you will need to have the hems lifted.

- If pants are pulling horizontally sideways at the leg crease, they are too tight around the butt and you need a larger size.

- If skirts or pants are too wide at the waist, you will need to take them in or have darts added.

By measuring yourself properly in the first place and understanding these guidelines, you are much more likely to find well-fitting clothes. Having an item of clothing that fits the wider sections of your body, and then altering the garment so that it is less boxy by taking it in at the sides, will make you feel more comfortable and look more stylish. The most spectacularly made designer outfit won't do you justice if it doesn't fit properly.

One of the golden rules of styling is a proper fit. Not only will you look better in figure-flattering, well-fitting clothes, your clothes will appear to be higher quality. Like a relationship with a person who is your perfect fit, it just works, it feels comfortable. Everybody sees it (and secretly longs for the same perfect fit in their life).

A great relationship may not start off fitting perfectly. However, if you truly like what you see, and the other person has enough room within them to make adjustments; ultimately, you can have a perfect fit. With someone who doesn't have enough give in them, you'll always feel uncomfortable and frustrated. It's the same with clothing.

Ultimately, alterations need to be seen as an essential ingredient of clothes buying.

It is easier to take an item of clothing in than it is to widen or lengthen it, due to a very small seam allowance. If you believe that a garment will be too tight in a rounder area of your body, such as bust, belly, hips or butt, it is always a better option to go up a size and alter down.

Below are some basic alterations you can do to maximise the fit of your garment, without breaking the bank.

ADJUSTMENTS AND ALTERATIONS

1. Hemming pants, skirts and dresses: when any of these items fit well everywhere else, adjusting the length will provide more wearability for your garment. This can be done by hand if you're good with a needle and thread. Otherwise, this is a simple and budget-friendly alteration that you could easily have done professionally.

2. Raise the hems of your tops: if your legs appear shorter than the rest of your body whenever you try on a particular top, shortening it to the hip or just above is a simple and inexpensive fix.

3. Take in waistlines on pants and skirts: curvy women with smaller waists than hips and thighs will often find that pants and skirts don't sit properly at the waistline. Taking the garment in an inch or more can make a huge difference to comfort and fit. If you find a skirt swirls around because it's too wide for your waist, the addition of a couple of darts will help to anchor it in place.

4. Take in tops, jackets, and dresses: this is a great adjustment for women who struggle to find clothes that fit them around the wider areas of their body. If a top fits comfortably around your bust or shoulders, but then falls straight down in a non- figure-enhancing box shape, this is the alteration that will bring the word svelte back into your wardrobe. By taking the sides of a garment in an inch or two you can have a more form-fitting top, dress or jacket.

5. Shorten the shoulder straps of tops and dresses: if your straps are too long then the garment will either sit too low on the décolletage or it will make it look as if you have nothing to fill the space. Shortening the shoulder straps will provide a more figure-hugging form.

SCALE

Why is scale important when it comes to your outfit selection? If a tall person stands next to someone who is short, each appears respectively taller and shorter due to their relative scales. You end up focusing on the height imbalance rather than on the people.

However, put a medium-height person next to either of them and the difference won't be as obvious. Put two tall people together and you start focusing more on the two people themselves. Put two petite people together and the same occurs.

Think about scale whenever you choose outfits, in relation to print size, or any form of accessory: jewellery, watches, bags, bracelets, rings, shoes and even pockets. If you are petite and choose to wear a larger chunky necklace, it will overwhelm your smaller features, taking the attention away from them, rather than harmonising with your face and décolletage and enhancing you. It's the equivalent of wearing something three sizes too big for you when you walk into a boutique. You wouldn't choose to do that with your clothing, so it's not the best thing to do when choosing your accessories either. If you have dainty thin wrists, small hands and delicate facial features, accessories that are dainty, thin and fine will suit you better than large pieces.

Someone with bigger lips, larger eyes or nose, needs a larger pendant to harmonise and balance their features. They also need larger prints in their outfits and larger details in general when it comes to their accessories. This works with glasses, bags, shoes, bracelets, watches and rings.

You may find that you have a fairly standard body size, with one area proportionately larger or smaller than the rest. For example, you might find that you have relatively thicker ankles and calves but that the rest of your body looks balanced. In this case, it would be good to wear chunkier-heeled or wedge-type shoes. A thin stiletto heel against a wider ankle and calf would only highlight the disproportion. Conversely, someone with a thinner ankle would appear clunky in a thicker heel.

The one thing, however, that overrides all rules of scale is personality! You may have all the fashion rules down pat when it comes to the perfect fit, body proportions and scale for your silhouette, but ultimately your personality is the most important element in aligning your style with the real you. When you really understand who you are and how you want to turn up in the world, authentic presentation is inevitable. Understanding your personality allows you to tie all of your styling knowledge together with the binding force of your personal creativity.

Chapter 18

Showing Up and Your Sense of Style

How you show up in life is your personal visual communication billboard. Your attire lets everyone around you know your values: how grounded or creative you may be, how much you like to be noticed or whether you're more a fan of how your clothing feels.

It really does seem a lot easier at times to just throw on a t-shirt and a pair of jeans and be done with all this dressing business. I mean, it's what is on the inside that counts, isn't it?

Naturally, what is on the inside counts significantly. Your radiance emanates from within. Nothing can compare with the twinkle in your eye, the warmth of your smile, the kindness of your words or actions, the compassion you bring to those around you or the gentleness of your touch.

However, if you have read this far, your personal style matters to you . As mentioned at the beginning of this book, I wanted this to be more than just a standard styling manual.

So instead of trying to pigeonhole you into a particular style category, I aim to empower you to develop your own unique expression by giving you an understanding of the principles of art and composition and how these relate to personal styling.

Don't worry if you've never picked up a pencil or paint brush in your lifetime. You won't need to here. What you're about to learn are the fundamentals of what makes an artwork a successful piece (things such as design principles) and then apply that knowledge to yourself. Instead of creating an artwork with a traditional canvas, set of paints and paint brushes, you're going to replace the traditional canvas with you. Your body, your face, your hair.

1. TONE AND COLOUR

In a painting class, you'll generally be asked to block in **TONE** first. The use of tone allows you to decide how much of your artwork is dark or light in value. *Tone* can be light, medium or dark, and is produced by the addition of grey to any colour (also called *HUE.*)

The way you lay out your tones on your canvas will give your artwork TONAL VALUE (how dark or light things are) as well as TONAL CONTRAST (the difference between light and dark between parts of a composition.)

A strong contrast between your light and dark tones will create a strong visual impact.

If your tones are all fairly similar then there is less visual impact from colour, and you may instead want to create impact through things like texture, line, and so forth.

In the case of fashion, this would mean playing with accessories, linework, sheen, fabric texture, prints and patterns.

Now let's look at how tone and tonal contrast relate to you and your personal appearance. When you select clothing or makeup, paying particular attention to a colour and the level of contrast it has against your natural skin tone, hair and eyes will have a strong impact on how good it looks on you.

Back to the mirror you go!

I want you to look very closely at your hair, skin and eye colour.

Is there a strong contrast, for example, between the lightness of your skin and the darkness of your hair?

If you were painting a picture of yourself and were asked to block in the dark, medium and light areas of your face, eyes, skin and eyebrows, would there be strong differences between areas of dark and light in this painting? What would be the darkest parts?

Would most of your artwork be covered in medium to light tones?

CHOOSING YOUR COLOUR PALETTE

I will be simplifying the colour analysis palettes into the basic autumn, winter, summer and spring palettes in this book. I am aware of (and use) a more extensive colour analysis method with my clients. This information, however, is beyond the scope of this book; the following information is here as a basic guide to help your understanding of warm and cool palettes, as well as tonal contrast.

WARM SKINTONE - STRONG TONAL CONTRAST

Below is an example of someone with medium-to-strong tonal contrast between her eye, skin and hair colour.

Notice her deeper-toned hair colour in contrast to a very pale skin colour and light-to-medium eye colour tone. The contrast is visually striking, which means that she can wear brighter or more saturated colours than most. Just take a look at how well the bright warm red lipstick works on her. The strength of the red lipstick comes from the contrast to her fair skin.

She is a classic example of warm colouring. Think of warm sunsets and the fiery reds, oranges, yellows and even browns of autumn leaves. She sits at the warmer end of the colour wheel, which means that everything on the right of the line in the illustration below, generally looks good on her.

This doesn't mean that someone with warm colouring can't wear greens, blues or violets. It just means that their greens, blues and violets will have a warmer base to them; for example, olive green has a warmer base to it than its cooler emerald green counterpart; ultramarine blue is a warmer red-based blue than, for example, cobalt or Prussian blue; and violets will once again be more red-based than blue-based.

People with autumn colouring tend to have warmer skin; their hair can be medium to very dark brown (throwing off copper/red hues) or medium to deep red (which can throw off golden or red undertones); and their eye colour can be medium-black brown, hazel, warm green or olive.

The colour palette below has resulted from blending the colours on the right of the colour wheel with different quantities of white, grey and black.

Many of the shades in this palette would suit as eyeshadows also for someone with an autumn colouring.

☙ Showing Up and Your Sense of Style ☙

Autumn Colour Palette:

Below are examples of warm-coloured tones that work well as lipsticks and blush colours. Notice how warm-coloured reds have more of an orange base to them, whereas once you pass the true red section (the middle colour) of the chart we start to see what happens to the red with the addition of blue.

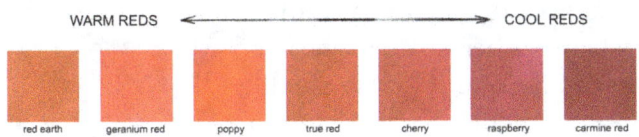

The temperature changes from warm to cool. Therefore, you want to stick to wearing shades that have more warmth in them (orange-based reds, pinks and browns).

Best neutrals: Chocolate, Army Green, Dark Caramel

Best metallics: Gold

WINTER SKINTONE

Now let's compare this lady with another person who has strong tonal contrast between her eye, hair and skin colour, only this time, we will be looking at someone who has more of a cool-toned colouring.

You can see that she has a very strong tonal contrast between her dark hair and her light skin colour and eyes. However, unlike our earlier autumn model, her hair has more of a jet black (blue-based) colouring to it. Her skin is more porcelain in appearance, which also has more of a cool, blue base to it. This means that when she looks for lipstick colours, for example, she needs to look for reds (such as the one she is wearing) that are blue-based (in other words, a lipstick that has a slight amount of blue added to true red) rather than orange-based (such as fire-engine red).

So, if we look back at the colour wheel to see where she would draw her best colours from, we will be looking on the left side of the wheel, where the cool blues, greens and yellows lie. This is not to say that you can't have any reds or pinks that are cool. It just means that yellows will be closer to lemon yellow (which has a cooler base) than to, say, an Indian Yellow (which has more of a warm, orange base to it). Any pinks/reds will tend to be more blue-based also, as mentioned above.

With such strong cool tonal contrasts between her hair, skin and eye colour, she would be best suited to wearing colours found in the winter colour palette below as these have the saturation of pigment (colour) her natural colouring and tonal contrast requires.

People with winter colour palettes tend to have brown, black, grey blue (slate), clear blue, or emerald green eyes and ashy mid-brown, dark brown, or black hair.

Winter Colour Palette:

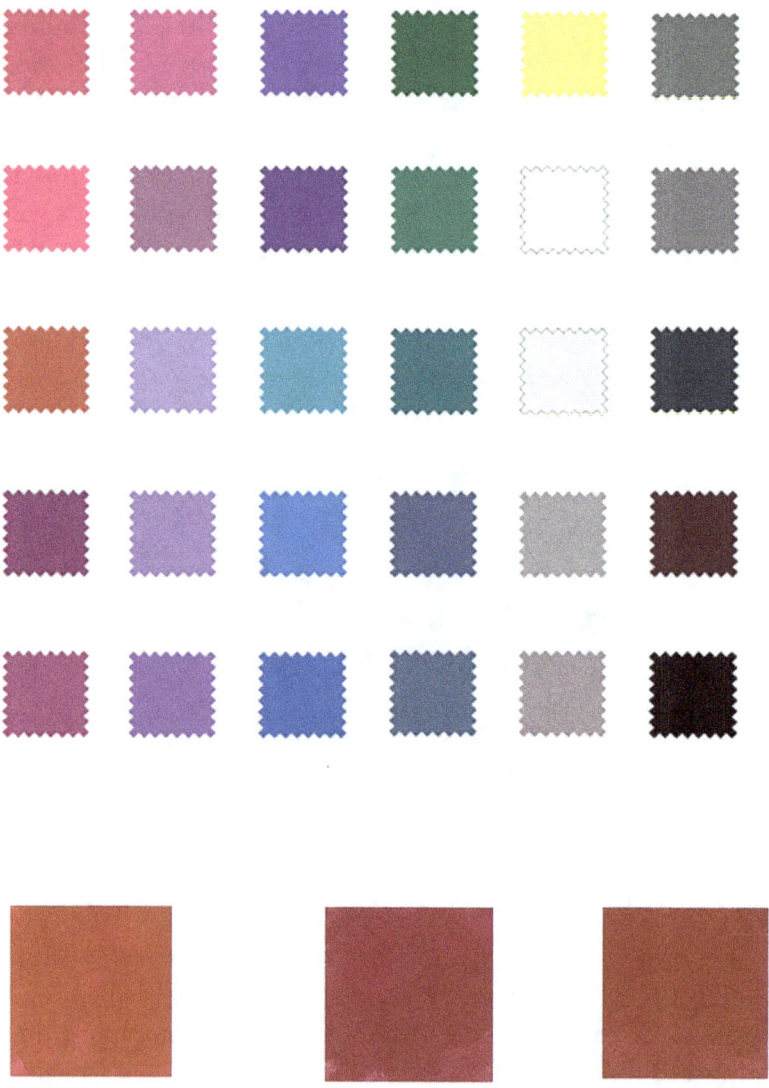

Above, you can see that colours such as cherry, raspberry and carmine red are all great lipstick colour choices for the winter palette, and a lot of the pinks from the winter colour palette will better suit this skin tone as blushes or lipsticks.

Best Neutrals: Black, Navy, Charcoal Grey

Best metallic highlight colours: Silver

WHEN TO LOOK FOR DEEPER VERSUS LIGHTER VERSIONS OF COLOURS

Look for deeper or lighter versions of a colour dependent on how light or dark your skin, hair and eyes are.

If you have darker skin, darker hair and darker eyes, then you should wear makeup (such as lipstick) that is a deeper shade of the base colour.

A SHADE is the addition of black to any colour. So, if you have a darker skin colour, hair and eyes, you will look better wearing a deeper burgundy lipstick colour over, say, a pale pink lipstick. Recognizing whether you have a warmer or cooler skin tone needs to be factored into your colour assessment also. Similarly, with clothing, wearing pastels won't harmonise as well with your skin if you have deeper and darker tones in your skin and hair as they won't harmonise with your depth of colour.

The same happens in reverse. If you have lighter hair, skin and eye colouring and there is very little contrast in tone between your hair, skin and eyes, then wearing a very saturated colour, such as deep purple, close to your face, will make it look like the colour is wearing you rather than you wearing the colour. People will look at the deeper shade of purple that you are wearing first and then at your face, instead of seeing you as a whole. Wearing a paler version of the purple colour, such as mauve, would suit you a lot more in this instance.

Adding more white to a colour is called creating a TINT of that colour. Pastel colours are examples of tints. The fairer you are, the more harmonious you will look in lighter colours.

Below is a chart showing SHADES and TINTS of red. As you can see, the more white that is added, the more the original red colour looks like pink (it was tinted with white), whereas the more black that was added to the red, the deeper the red colour looks (it was shaded with black.)

Below are examples of more TINTED versions of both warm and cool colour schemes and whom they suit.

WARM SKINTONE - LOW TONAL CONTRAST

When you move out of winter, you are moving out of a cooler season and back into more warmth. Warm sunlight is a great way to visualize how lightening or tinting a warm set of colours can alter how they appear. Rather than the deeper, earthier tones of autumn, spring colours are lighter and sunnier.

Adding tint takes the depth out of the base colour and makes it appear less intense with this colour palette. This means that the spring colour palette would best suit someone with less contrast in their hair, skin and eyes.

Spring Colour Palette:

Below is an example of someone with a lighter warm colouring.

Someone with this colouring has lighter hair (it may be light, strawberry blonde, or golden). In this case it is golden blonde, which is a light version of a warm colour. There is warmth in her skin; however, there is minimal contrast as far as tonal value goes. Her eye colouring (which may be clear blue, turquoise green, hazel, or light brown) is a similar tone to her skin and hair.

Therefore, when selecting makeup, lipstick shades and outfits, you will be looking for warm colours that are more muted so that they don't dominate you.

Below are great examples of lipstick and blush shades that would suit a spring colour tone. As you can see, they are all quite warm yet light. Remember that nudes are your friend.

☙ Showing Up and Your Sense of Style ☙

NEUTRALS ARE YOUR FRIEND

Instead of washing you out, neutral warm colours enhance you because they harmonise with the low contrast levels in your skin, hair and eyes.

Dusty pinks and beige colours also work well with this skin tone.

Best Metallic highlight colours:
Bronze

For a bit of bling, you can rock a bronze-coloured metallic either on your eyelids as eyeshadow or on shoes, belts, tops, etc.

MEDAL BRONZE
PANTONE 17-0942
PAPER SET

Best neutrals: Warm Grey, Olive, Camel

≈ Showing Up and Your Sense of Style ≈

COOL SKINTONE - LOW TONAL CONTRAST

Now let's look at what happens when you add extra white/light to a cool colour palette. Summer is the brightest season of the year. The light dominates the sky for longer hours of the day. Likewise, the addition of white to cooler colours means that pastels abound in this colour palette.

Once again, we are looking at someone with minimal tonal contrasts between their hair, skin and eye colours. In this case you will often see women with more of an ash blonde to medium brown hair colouring, pale eyes (blue, cool green, grey-brown, grey-blue, or slate) and fair skin (with more of a rosy base).

◅⁓ When Glamour Meets Gratitude ⁓▻

Therefore, when selecting makeup, lipstick shades, and outfits, you will be looking for cool colours with the addition of white to them. Otherwise, they will dominate your look.

Below are great examples of eyeshadows and blush shades that would suit a summer colour tone.

Best Lipstick colours: Powder Pink, Rose Pink, Dusty Pink, Cranberry, Mauve

Best Neutrals: Greys (blue-based), Cool Taupe and Slate Blue

Best metallic highlight colour: platinum

HOW TO USE TONE IN YOUR OUTFITS

Where you decide to place darker tones and where you choose to place lighter tones will have a significant impact on how your silhouette appears, how people's eyes will travel around your body when they look at you and how much focus they will put on different parts of you.

When organizing your outfit, know that lighter tones in jewelry, shoes, belts, scarves, tops, pants, jackets and so forth will make that area of the body come forward. So, if you want to bring more attention to a particular area, wearing a lighter-coloured tone on that section of your body will make it advance visually. Wearing a mid-tone will allow the eye to travel harmoniously over that section of the body without really feeling the need to linger. Wearing a darker tone in a particular section of the body will make the area recede visually. Therefore, if you have a larger butt or hips that you want to make appear visually slimmer, you may want to place darker tones in that section of the body in contrast with lighter tones farther up the body where you may be naturally slimmer.

Remember that your makeup, hair and clothes colour choices are the equivalent of choosing the correct colour of paint to apply to a canvas. Not only do you need to select clothes, makeup and hair colours carefully, but you also need to recognize the canvas you are working with.

The most important focal points of your body/canvas when it comes to styling are your shoulders, your bust line, your waist and your hips. The outline they create will give you an understanding of your silhouette.

Take a look at these areas and ask yourself the following questions:

Shoulders

1. Are my shoulders in line with my hips? Then you have a balanced silhouette.
2. Are my shoulders wider than my hips? Then you have broad shoulders.
3. Are my shoulders narrower than my hips? Then you have narrow shoulders.

Bust

4. Does my bust take up significant space on my torso? Then you would want to downplay this section.
5. Is my bust small or large relative to my hips?
6. Does my bust outline (silhouette) line up with my hips?

Waist

7. Is my waistline noticeably slimmer than the rest of my body? Then you can draw attention to your slim waistline.
8. Is my waistline slimmer, the same or wider than the area directly beneath my bustline?
9. Am I short-waisted or do I have a long torso. You would downplay a shorter waist and emphasize the waistline of a longer torso.

Hips/thighs

10. Are my hips/thighs visibly wider than my shoulders? You would generally (but not always) aim to decrease attention to the thighs and hips and add more detail to the shoulders in order to balance out this shape.

11. Are my hips/thighs narrower than my shoulders? You can add more detail and lighter tones to the hips and thighs to balance out the shoulder-to-hip ratio.

By answering these questions, you are able to establish your body's structure. This could be compared to selecting the size and shape of the canvas you wish to paint on.

Now you can go back to the outfit you laid out on your bed and see how well it would work on your body (your canvas). Do you need darker tones on the lower, mid or upper part of your body? Do you need to add darker tones on the outer section of your body (through the use of jackets/cardigans) or do you want the centre of your body to appear more elongated and slim (through the use of one solid dark tone)?

Below are examples of how silhouettes appear when the outfit focuses on tone as its main element.

Here we see a woman dressed in a monochromatic colour scheme (meaning the same colour with only white and black added to it) that utilizes tone as its main element (along with the texture of her jacket).

She has visually broken her body up into very distinguishable areas—light, medium and dark tones of the same colour. The eye immediately travels to the lightest section—her top—and sees the contrast of the jacket and skirt. Having these distinct tonal blocks in place draws your eye to the upper part of the body. The darker jacket keeps everything enclosed or contained underneath, like a wrapping of sorts.

Just remember when you are playing with light to dark tones that greater contrast between tones means a greater visual impact. If all of the tones are a similar strength, you tend to look at the body as a whole, whereas when there is stronger contrast, the eye will visually break up the body. This can be a good thing or a not-so-good thing depending on who is wearing it and why.

This leads me on to discussing **columns of colour** and how to maximise their use.

In the illustration below, you can see that the darkest colour is placed in the central section of the body—in other words, from shoulder line to the ankles; and this is positioned next to a jacket in a slightly lighter tone. This makes the jacket advance and the body recede. Wearing a **column of colour** means the eye can travel up and down the body without having to pause. If you're a petite person, you generally want to keep the body free of tonal breaks. You want the eye to travel up the body and see it as a whole. This has an elongating effect on the petite silhouette. This includes the colour of your shoes and how it connects to the leg or pant colour.

Wearing *a darker column of colour in the centre of the body* also has a slimming effect here and is an ideal choice for anyone wanting to downplay a larger belly or wider middle section.

Alternatively, you may want to slim down your hips, thighs and butt. If this is the case, you could choose to place the *darker column of colour on the outer parts of your body*. The darker tones push back and enclose the body's edges with, for example, the use of a matching darker-toned jacket and pants or skirt and a lighter-toned blouse underneath the outer layer. The lighter tone brings the attention up towards the face and in towards the centre of the body, whilst the darker tones used on the outside of the body visually push back its edges.

From here on in, I would like you to think about how the use of TONE will affect your SHAPE each time you select or lay out an outfit.

BLEND

As mentioned previously, not everyone has enough tonal contrast in their personal colouring to be able to wear a lot of saturated colour or colour contrasts; however, this doesn't stop you from being able to blend a lighter and a darker colour together with the addition of accessories, the lightening or darkening of hair colour, or by wearing particular shades of lipstick and eyeshadow.

Not everyone suits harsh lines in their tonal contrast between deeper and lighter tones of colour. With summer and spring skin tones, there is little tonal contrast between the hair, skin and eyes. Therefore, strong colour near or on the face (with, for example, the use of lipstick colours that are too deep or saturated) can mean that the colour wears them rather than them wearing the colour.

A winter or autumn skin tone will wear strong tonal contrasts in the colours in their outfits much better than their summer and spring counterparts. However, they won't be able to wear pastels or nudes with the same elegance or enthusiasm.

At the end of it all, style is constantly striving for BALANCE and HARMONY, just like nature.

However, this doesn't mean you can't change up that balance. If you are naturally very fair and have minimal contrast in your hair, skin and eyes then this doesn't often allow for much play room when it comes to how saturated a pigment you can wear.

However, if you want bolder contrasts and more saturated colour in your life but your natural colouring doesn't allow it, you could potentially ask your colourist to darken your hair. Start with two shades and darken progressively as this will help you adjust yourself, your wardrobe and your makeup to the change. You will need to start looking for deeper/brighter shades of colours you already successfully wear in your wardrobe for this to be a successful change. You will need to start experimenting with bolder lip colours than you previously did. Alternatively, you may go for brighter shades of eyeshadow than you previously wore.

The opposite applies for lightening your hair. If you choose to lighten your hair, you will find that you will probably need to find more mid-toned or lighter tints of the colours you previously wore. This will apply to your lipstick and eyeshadow colour selection also—think nuder or more pastel colours dependent on whether you are a warm- or cool- based colouring.

If you feel that changing your hair colour is too dramatic and scary but you really like the light-colour top you laid out and it just isn't blending in properly with your deeper warm skin tone, then the addition of a darker-coloured necklace, pendant, earrings, blazer, cardigan, or a scarf folded and tied around the hairline can be the blending tool that will allow you to wear that nuder colour more successfully.

The same thing goes in reverse. If you have a lighter skin tone that suits pastels and you want to wear a saturated bold colour near your neckline, your skin will be overwhelmed by the colour. People will be looking at your top before they look at you. "But I love that colour," I hear you say. Then ask yourself how you can blend this colour to your face. Is there a mid-lighter version of that tone that you can find in your scarf, necklace, earrings or jacket that will help you blend the strength of that coloured top into the face in a more gradual and flattering way?

And you might ask yourself these same questions if you see a harsh demarcation around your waist or hiplines with tops and skirts. Do you want such an obvious tonal contrast between both areas, or do you want to graduate the contrast? If you want the column of colour contrast to work properly then yes, you do want a stronger contrast. However, if you don't want a strong horizontal division of the body through tonal contrast, then consider blending with belts, cardigans, bracelets and bags, or even the choice of colour you use on your top and bottom half.

2. DIRECTION/LINE

The next stage of this exercise is to work out where you want the eye to move around the outfit based on the use of line in the garment.

Even your hair and makeup are impacted by the use of line. A strong cat flick on the top lash line will have a framing effect on the upper lash line. The thickness and intensity of colour you choose for your eyeliner will have a definite impact on how much attention gets drawn to your eyes.

Your **eyebrows**, when well-groomed in the way they are shaped, how thick or thin they are, and how much they are filled in or coloured, will create different lines and angles around the eyes and once again frame the face and eyes.

Mascara or false lashes frame the eyes. This attention to detail on a line—in this case the **lash line**—will increase our attention to the eyes and the colour and intended shape we wish to create.

With regards to hair, even the way your **hair is parted** or the addition of a **fringe** (or bangs) will create lines that affect the overall shape of your face (see the earlier chapter on hairstyles for face shapes).

In clothing, vertical, horizontal and diagonal lines have a strong effect on how our eyes travel and can break up or slim down a body. The width of the line also affects how quickly or slowly our eyes move over a section of the body.

Details on clothes such as buttons, zippers, pockets, fringing, darts, seams, pleats, collars, lapels and necklines can create vertical, diagonal or horizontal lines on the parts of the body these lay on.

Below are some examples of line used in different outfits. These lines have been placed strategically on certain sections of the body in the design of the outfit. Notice how they affect the wearer based on where they are positioned.

Line: A horizontal line that sits above the bustline draws attention to the shoulder line making them look wider than what they actually are. The eyes will then travel upwards towards the face. A horizontal line can also be created by off-the-shoulder tops and dresses.

Horizontal lines that run from shoulder line to under the bustline will create more attention to this area. The horizontals at this area will help to widen it visually. Therefore, if you have a smaller bust, then finding a top with a line created through two pockets, a flap, frills, or alternating horizontal lines at this area will help to make your bust look larger.

Compare this to a line that sits under the bust line. Here we see that the line draws attention from under the bust line and flares out from this section. The placement of what is known as an empire line in dresses or blouses helps to create a false waist for non-waisted shapes. If you have a more rectangular waistline or a waistline that is wider than your bust, then an empire line is a much better alternative than standard cinched-in waisted styles.

This is because the area under your bust is often the slimmest area for someone with a wider waist. Making this a focal point on the body of someone with a wider waist or larger belly gives the body more curve.

If your waist is the smallest part of you then the most flattering thing to do for your body shape is to draw attention to it by creating a horizontal line there with a belt.

A horizontal line created closer to the hip bone will bring attention down past the waist. This is an ideal line to create if you have a shorter waist and longer legs. You can create this line with a belt that sits below the waistline, by wearing lower-waisted pant styles or by stopping jackets below the hip bone. It also works well on figures that have less natural curve, such as the rectangular silhouette, as it creates a false waistline.

Horizontal line or lines at the thighs. These often occur as ruffled or tiered skirts. You may find pockets, fringing and horizontal lines in this area. If you have slimmer thighs and hips in relation to your shoulders it is a good idea to wear horizontal lines here to balance out your silhouette.

Vertical lines

Now let's look at what happens when you apply vertical lines to your outfits.

Here you can see how the outfit on the left creates a black vertical line in the centre with lighter vertical lines created by the jacket colour. This creates an elongating effect on the body and helps to make the belly and waist area appear slimmer.

The vertical lines created in the image on the right show the black lines slimming down the outer edges of the body, with more attention paid in the central panel.

Women with a larger bust will benefit from necklines with a small slit in the centre of the chest. Bringing your attention to the centre of the body will stop you from reading the bust area as one wide band. The slit vertically positioned scarf, plunging necklace or zipper helps to cut through the roundness of the bust and break up this area.

Vertical seams that run through the bust or just under the bust have a slimming effect also, as they cut through the bust and waist, which elongates this area.

Darts added into shirts, tops and dresses around the bust area help to mould the outfit to a woman's contours instead of making the garment hang too widely. And even though a dart is primarily used to create a better fit, it still creates a vertical line in the clothing and slims the body in doing so.

Vertical darts help to mould the outfit to a person's contours. The reduction of fabric in this process has a slimming effect.

Narrow vertical stripes in blouses are more elongating and slimming. Wider stripes are more widening.

Below we see the elongating effect that the vertical lines create when worn in either skirts or pants from the waist down. This is an ideal line to wear if you have shorter legs. Just ensure that you do choose designs with vertical lines that are spaced closely together, as a wider vertical line can create more width.

Below we see a brilliant example of vertical side panels in a dress that run from the lower bust line. Such panels/lines work to create a slimming effect on her hips and thighs as they visually cut through the roundness of the hips and thighs. If she had a larger waist and belly, this would also be hidden by the vertical side panels (similar to how a cardigan or jacket hides curves).

Now let's observe the *difference between vertical and horizontal lines* on the body.

The thinner the vertical line, the more of a slimming/elongating effect it has and the faster the eyes will travel down the area.

Compare the above dress to the following dress, which is covered in horizontal lines. Notice the widening effect it has on its wearer.

Diagonal Lines

Let's look at some examples of diagonal lines in garments. V-necks on a dress, top, blouse or jacket help to take away the bulk of the bust area. Look specifically for diagonals created with jacket lapels that start from and button under the breast.

A diagonal line across the shoulders slims down the shoulder line because it cuts across the width of the area.

Many halter neck designs create a similar effect to the raglan sleeve style in that they cut through the width of the broader shoulders with diagonal lines.

Wrap dresses create a beautiful silhouette as they cut through the bust area and waist and are also great for bringing the eye inward to the center of the body. This dress style flatters pretty much all body types.

Diagonal lines in both pants and skirts have a thigh-slimming effect on the wearer.

Aside from its slimming effect, a diagonal line creates more interest in an area.

It may create an alternate hem line to the standard horizontal, which is a lot more fun. Whether it's a diagonal fold of the clothing, flap or zipper, diagonals make the eye stop and look again—lots of fun for the wearer and the observer.

Curved lines

We can recreate similar effects of the vertical lengthening, diagonal interest, or horizontal widening only with a rounded, feminine impact.

For example, instead of a V-neck diagonal line, you might prefer a sweetheart neckline. Both have a flattering effect on the bustline, but one is more rounded and feminine.

Scooped necklines and **cowl necklines** are other examples of how a low curved line can help to reduce the appearance of a larger bust. This is also something you can recreate with necklaces also.

Scoop neckline　　　　Cowl neckline　　　　Scoop necklace style

However, you will notice that the higher your rounded neckline is around the neck, the larger your bust will appear. This is great for those with smaller busts, so a **curved crew neckline** or a shorter, rounded necklace is something to consider if you have a small bust.

Another thing to consider is the hemline of your tops. A curved hemline is a lot more flattering than a straight horizontal line. A horizontal line will make your eye stop at its end point, causing you to notice the width of a thicker waist or larger tummy and butt. However, with a rounded hemline, your eye curves around the front of the body and cuts up into the hips and thighs, whilst your waist, tummy and butt are sufficiently covered. The curved hemline is a winner on all body shapes.

If you have curves at your hips/thighs and want to find jeans that fit, look for ones that have curved side seams rather than straight side seams for a better fit.

3. PRINTS /PATTERN

It is important to look for a couple of elements when choosing a print:

1. How large or small the print is in scale (relative to your own personal scale).
2. Where the print detail lies on your actual body.

We've spoken about scale earlier on in the chapter called "Fitting In and Measuring Up." However, the location of print detail on your body when you wear the garment is often overlooked. This is a critical factor in deciding the suitability of the print selection.

Let's imagine you have broad shoulders and decide to wear a large bold print that has the majority of its design along the shoulder line, bust and back itself. As beautiful as the print may be, you'll find yourself avoiding the garment because it makes your shoulders look wider, purely because the emphasis will be drawn to this area.

The same would go for a print that has a design that features at the hemline of your shirt and which ends at your hips. Imagine now that you want to de-emphasize your hips. A top with the majority of the print design sitting around the hips will only draw attention to this section of your body and make it look wider.

Not to worry, though, because the same rules that apply to line apply to print. If you have a small bust, you can use a print with a pattern that sits horizontally across the bust to your benefit.

Here we can see that the print follows the direction of the wrap top's diagonal lines. This has a slimming effect at the waistline.

You may want to add width to the hips and thighs. Prints that run in horizontal lines are great for this.

Or, you may want to define the waist as the smallest point and then highlight the curves of your hips and thighs with a print such as this one.

If you have a shorter waist and longer legs and you want to bring people's attention down, you could choose a skirt that has stronger parts of the print detail towards the hem of the skirt.

To help visually widen the legs, you may want to try a print that runs in horizontal lines across the trouser.

Most of all, have fun with your prints. They're there to add interest and fun to your wardrobe.

4. TEXTURE

When it comes to your personal appearance, texture plays a huge part. Let's take a look at images of the same women with curly hair, wavy hair and straight hair. The straighter or smoother the hair, the more structured and sleek the look. The wavier or curlier the hair, the more feminine and romantic the look. Curly hair also adds more volume around the face.

When it comes to makeup application, you may want a **matte** foundation together with lipstick that is shine-free in texture, thicker, fuller coverage and longer-wearing.

Alternatively, there are **satin** finish foundations and lipsticks. These are medium-weight and medium-yet-buildable coverage foundations that give the skin a natural glow. A satin lipstick is creamier in its texture.

Finally, you may prefer a more **dewy**, lightweight foundation with a **glossy** lip finish. This foundation finish is a lot shinier and best suited for younger skins with minimal breakout.

Matte finish

Satin Finish

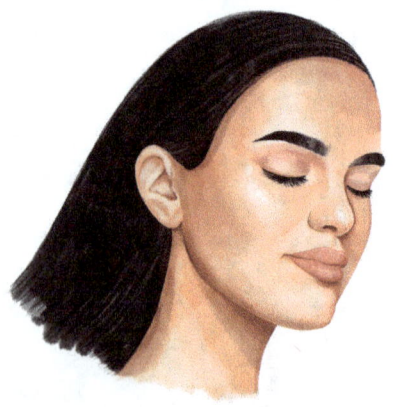

Dewey/Gloss finish

Then we see **texture in clothing.**

Texture can be seen in the type of fabric you choose to wear. It stimulates our sense of sight and touch, whereas a lot of the earlier elements of composition only stimulated our sense of sight.

Texture is where clothes designers really get to play with the use of beading, sequins, tassels, fringing, feathers, baubles, bows, fur, wool, satin, silk, pleats, lace and ruffles.

Below are a number of images that display different examples of texture in fashion. It is unlikely that you will be able to wear such extreme uses of texture in your day-to-day lifestyle; however, a sequined top, a scarf that has faux fur trim, a dress with fringing or the addition of lace around the neckline can all work to create more interest in your outfit.

Ultimately, the use of texture in your outfit is not only something that might feel nice to the touch or be strategically placed in your outfit to add bulk to an area you feel needs extra volume—texture is also fun. This is where you can really unleash your creativity and play.

◅ When Glamour Meets Gratitude ▻

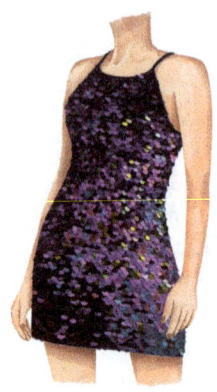  

Now go back to the outfit you have laid out on the bed and see whether you can add texture anywhere on your outfit. This may be the addition of a textured scarf, beaded jewelry, a shirt with tassels on its hem or a crossover cardigan with ruffles on its edging—whatever lights you up and adds a little extra dimension to your look is ideal. Better still, position the texture strategically to help add volume to areas of the body that might be in need.

5. ACCENT/HIGHLIGHTS

Like the bow on a freshly wrapped present, you want to finish off and wrap up your outfit with a little accent.

Now your **accent** can be anything from an amazing handbag to a bright scarf, sparkly necklace, fun brooch, jingly bangle or metallic shoes.

Do you want your accent piece to be up around your face, hair or neckline? Or do you want it to be brought down to the wrist—perhaps a belt? Or do you want us to see your favourite new shoes?

Is there a focal point you want to draw our attention towards? Or do you want multiple highlight points with varying levels of oomph?

Your **highlights,** on the other hand, might also be added to entire sections of the body. You applied this principle in the tones section by looking for the area of the body you wished to highlight or widen and placing your lighter tone there.

When it comes to highlighting, you can add to this principle. By highlighting a section of your body, you distract attention away from areas of the body you are trying to camouflage.

Below we see a shimmery metallic top used as a focal highlight. This highlight placement is great for bringing attention upwards and is especially helpful for women who want to draw attention away from their hips or for petites.

However, not everyone can pull off shine and sequins across an entire section of their body. This is where accessories come in.

This is where we focus on the **accent** over the highlight, and this is where accessories become your best friend in tying your entire look together.

Accents for the hair

When it comes to the hair, an accent might be a headband, hair clip, ribbon, scarf or an interesting tie such as a bow.

Accents for the ears

We have discussed best earrings for each face shape at length in the chapter "Eyes, Ears and Brows," finding the right length of earring will help draw attention to the face as an overall shape, including the smile, or they will direct the attention to your eyes.

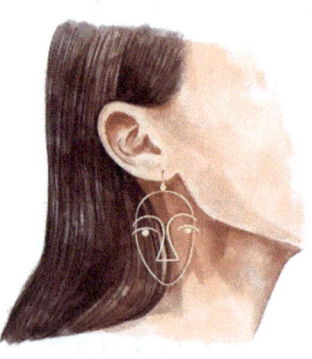

If you want to draw attention to the face as a whole, then wear longer earrings (such as long hoops), dangle earrings or drop styles that stop at or below the jawline.

If you wish to draw more attention to your eyes go for smaller earrings that stay close to the earlobes such as diamond studs or huggies.

☙ Showing Up and Your Sense of Style ☙

Accents for the face

Any girl who watches social media has seen the impact of a touch of highlight at the high points of the face, including the bridge of the nose, the tops of the cheekbones and the top of the cupid's bow.

The addition of strategically placed highlights (in conjunction with contour) adds more dimension to the face and adds light/brightness back to the face, giving the skin a more youthful glow/radiance.

(See the section on contouring and highlighting in the chapter on cheeks, nose and lips for more instructional information.)

Accents at the neckline

Now let's imagine you have a larger bust line that you want to draw less attention to.

Larger necklaces bring the attention to the center of the bust area. The necklaces need to be of a larger scale if you have a larger bust to match the scale of the bosom. Layers of necklaces work well for the larger neckline as you're visually cutting through a deeper amount of flesh.

Creating a diagonal line with the way you tie your scarf also helps to draw attention away from the bust line. An asymmetrical design breaks up the area it sits in. You also want to make sure that you tie the scarf lower down the chest area. If you tie it too close to the neck, it will create extra bulk in this area (for more detail read the chapter on scarves).

❦ Showing Up and Your Sense of Style ❦

However, if you are small-busted and want to create more volume here, how could you add an accent to make this area of the body appear more voluminous?

Necklaces that have multiple stands of finer beads will add visual bulk in this area, as will necklaces that land at the bust peak and spread out slightly.

A scarf works especially well to create visual bulk in the chest area. The most volume will be created in this area if you tie the scarf closer to the neckline.

Belts as accents

If you have a curvy body and your waist is the narrowest part of you, make sure to play this up with a wider belt that cinches in at the waist. Highlight, highlight, highlight your slim waist!

If you have a short torso and longer legs, then finding a belt that sits lower around the hips is a better option for you as it helps to visually elongate and balance out an otherwise shorter area. Alternatively, finding a belt in the same colour as your top will create a visual elongation of your torso.

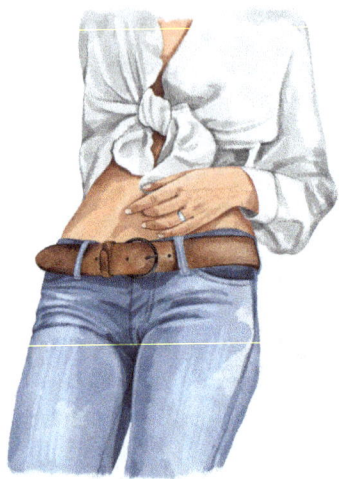

You also want to keep your belt positioned lower than the natural waistline if you have a full bust because larger breasts will visually shorten the mid-torso/waist area. Lower placement of the belt will create a visual elongation of the torso once again.

Alternatively, you may want to wear your belt above your natural waistline if your under bust measurement is narrower than your waist. This creates a false waist and a narrower focal point in the torso.

This will also give a lengthening effect to the legs as you are moving your perceived waistline upwards. This is therefore a great look for women with shorter legs.

Well-chosen bags are a finishing touch to your outfit.

For example, if you want to decrease the broadness of your shoulder line, then a bag that crosses over your body and ends at your hip creates an amazingly flattering diagonal line that visually slims down the upper torso. It also directs attention towards your hipline instead of your shoulders. This is a good thing as women with broader shoulders often have narrower hips proportionally.

If you have wider hips and don't want to draw extra attention here, then look for a shorter shoulder bag that ends higher than your hip as this will draw attention upwards.

Finally, there are the shoes. We have gone into detail about the different types of shoes you need to have in your closet; however, how do you know which shape of shoe will suit you?

If you have shorter legs, then you want to look for shoes that expose more of your feet (shoes that have a lower vamp). This adds to the visual length of your leg. If you wear straps at the ankle, it will create a horizontal line at the ankle that shortens the look of the leg.

Another thing to consider if you want to lengthen the look of your leg is pointier shoes. This, of course, is a matter of personal preference. However, a pointier shoe will add a little extra length to the leg line as a whole.

If you have wider calves and ankles, think NUDE! Ensure that you choose shoes that have a chunkier heel or platform. This will balance out the scale of the ankles and calves. If you go for something finer, it will make your legs look wider by comparison.

6. MOOD

Finally, I want you to look over your completed outfit. What does it reflect about your mood? Colour is one of the ways you can affect this.

What emotion or set of qualities are you portraying?

Are your accessories bright, colourful and fun?

Are they classic, refined and sophisticated?

Are they sharp, cutting-edge, geometric?

Are they feminine and soft with floral designs, soft and fluid or with rounded edges?

Are they more earthy, incorporating fringing or tassles or made from natural fibres?
Or are they loud, full of bling, screaming designer labels?

Everybody has a style or combination of styles that will set the mood for their outfit. If you look at your wardrobe there will generally be a handful of items that you absolutely love. It may be a blouse with ruffles and frills or tassels; it may be a particular dress because of the fabric quality or texture; it may be the fluid design of an outfit and how it hangs on your body; or it could be that you like a more tailored outfit. Whatever it is that you like about the piece, it will give your outfit a particular mood or convey something about you that, prior to really paying attention to this aspect of your wardrobe, you may have just selected unconsciously.

Regardless, there will be something about the design that catches your eye and makes you want to wear the item. However, for a composition to work it needs to be put together in a cohesive way. If you've ever walked into a house with a whole set of different themes running through it—for example, bits of coastal with bits of country cottage decor and French vintage with bits of contemporary and bits of Victorian era furnishings—the place starts to look cluttered and disjointed. There is nothing to tie the items together. However, if you have a couple of contemporary chairs mixed into a Victorian style apartment, you can make this design work. It's all about balance and harmony and understanding which items fit which style. The principles of design apply to all visual forms of communication. Your wardrobe is one of these.

Therefore, to maximize your wardrobe and tie it in with your hair and makeup effectively, you need to understand the story you wish to communicate about yourself with your outfit. The way you wish to express yourself. The aspects of yourself that most resonate with your sense of style and personality.

We can choose any style of attire. What we select, how we wear it, when we wear it and whether we wear it in a subdued or dramatic fashion (or anything in between) is totally up to you and the mood you're in when you select the item.

To really reflect the mood of your attire effectively, you need to ask yourself how you want your outfit to make you feel when you're wearing it.

Do you want to feel feminine, soft and romantic?

When thinking of the feminine, there is a feeling of softness. You will see this in the softness of fabrics and the softness of colour—often softer pastels are worn here.

The feminine is fluid and full. Think of the feminine energy of nature: a gentle breeze, water flowing in a stream.

Showing Up and Your Sense of Style

With this in mind, you will look for fluid shapes in design where the garment drapes, comes to a point and then flares out so that there is a soft flow of fabric that floats past.

The feminine is also into detail. Expect to find intricate and delicate embroidery in accessories and clothing alike. Jewelry is also more ladylike—for example, a delicate silver or gold bracelet.

Notice how there are lots of ruffles, bows, lace, floral prints, soft colours and flowy fabrics. These are a great way to tap into your femininity and glide through your day.

When it comes to the hair, feminine hair is generally longer, wavy-curly and worn out so that it can flow with the rest of you or pulled back with a ribbon or soft tie.

Brows are neatly shaped, and makeup is generally softer, with blushed cheeks, nude lipsticks and gentle colour washes across the eyelids.

 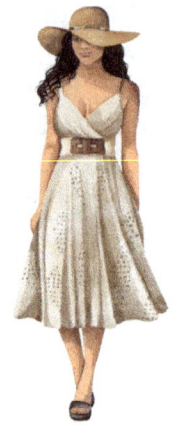 

Of course, this isn't the only way to connect to your feminine side. In the soft, romantic style we see a more airy quality. Next, I would like us to explore what happens when you add a more earthy essence to the feminine.

<u>Want to embrace your free spirited, earthy feminine side?</u>

Formerly known as hippie-styled dressing, this style has evolved into what is now known as Bohemian or **BOHO Chic**. Still feminine and romantic at its core, there is a touch of earthy spirituality to it, incorporating a relaxed, free-spirited groundedness to its vibe. Often associated with artists and independent thinkers, this style is open to and embraces many cultures and feminine clothing styles from across the globe. This can be seen in its eclectic layering and blending of patterns, textiles and colours.

This style celebrates long traditions of female crafts from around the globe, such as handstitching, embroidery, sewing and weaving techniques, crocheting, patchwork designs, the incorporation of tassels and fringing. It is a celebration of the worldwide female craftmakers and draws on style elements from various cultures, be they Mexican, Native American, Asian, or Oriental.

Showing Up and Your Sense of Style

Hair styles in this look are a combination of braids, loose waves and curls. Hair is longer or tossled and can be worn in an upstyle or down and flowing.

Brows are less defined and kept tidy but still maintain their natural shape. Makeup is generally quite natural and earthy tones are preferred.

Perhaps you want to convey vibrancy, creativity, playfulness with a touch (or punch) of drama?

<u>If quirky, fun and flamboyant are qualities you wish to embody:</u>

Look for fashion items that are fun, intensely colourful, carry extravagant prints and fascinate your senses with their design. "Exciting, flashy, striking and quirky" is what needs to be expressed through your outfits. Look for accessories that attract attention in a theatrical way.

This style of dressing shows reverence to colour combinations, with pattern on pattern placed together in a unique way; whether it's the choice of bold prints, whether it's the actual cut of the garment, or whether it's the colour and pattern or texture combinations. The flamboyant dresser is more daring and creative than most. Shoes are worn for impact not comfort, although they can be comfortable if you're wearing street wear.

Hair ranges from pixie cuts to waves. There are no rules here.

Showing Up and Your Sense of Style

Makeup ties in with the intense colour in outfits. Eye makeup is often more experimental around eyeshadow colours. Lip colour can be matched to the outfit.

Bear in mind that there are levels of the creative dresser out there. Some prefer to incorporate pattern on pattern into their style and others may just add in the accessories in a creative way. However, the important thing here is being able to wear your outfit in a different way and stand out from the crowd as unique.

Bit too over the top for your liking?

Perhaps you prefer a more refined, tailored look that has stood the test of time and is now considered classic.

If you want to feel more refined and classic, then nothing beats a high-quality tailored outfit made of the finest material.

As the classic style is more structured, hair worn with this style is often more polished. It is generally sleeker or blow dried. Makeup may be a perfectly applied winged liner and pink or red lipstick. Brows will be perfectly manicured, as will finger and toenails.

Accessories are of the finest quality and may be a string of pearls or a simple but select gold necklace, or a silk scarf.

Bags, belts, and shoes are also more structured and finely stitched. The look is one of simple sophistication and timeless elegance.

When Glamour Meets Gratitude

Too much effort maintaining a polished look?

Are you someone who would much prefer to just be comfortable in their daywear?

Do you want to feel relaxed, grounded and comfortable in your second skin?

If *casual* and *comfortable* are words and feelings that resonate with you, then embrace it with your wardrobe. It's especially important to feel this way if you know you'll be spending the day running around. The last thing you

Showing Up and Your Sense of Style

want to deal with are blisters. Find your favourite natural-fibred fabrics, add a pair of comfortable, well-fitting jeans and pop on a pair of ballet flats, canvas shoes or comfortable ankle boots, throw on a warm scarf, blazer or cardigan, grab your most practical bag and you're ready to move through your day with comfort as your guide.

Hair looks great pulled back in a ponytail or out as it falls.

Makeup? Maybe a lip gloss, a BB cream and mascara, but really, you're not wanting to spend too much time getting ready each morning.

Accessories: your practical handbag, comfortable shoes, a pair of sunglasses and a watch. Just the basics.

Comfortable is great for running around but your imagination keeps you wandering off to distant lands. How can you incorporate this into your style?

Do you want to travel to exotic lands and run wild?

Then perhaps a more exotic vibe is in order. You may find yourself attracted to silk scarves and animal prints, be they leopard, snakeskin or zebra-style prints. Oriental, Middle Eastern, African, South American. Anything that plays with colour and print and is unique. Whatever you wear, it will be eye-catching.

Perhaps you prefer larger earrings and colourful jewelry such as necklaces and bracelets that are a little more unique and eye-catching.

This woman is not afraid of makeup and uses it to enhance her exotic beauty, especially her eyes.

≈ Showing Up and Your Sense of Style ≈

Or perhaps you want to own your power. You've worked hard and you want people to see all that you've accomplished in life.

Do you want to tap into the DRAMATIC and powerful part of you?

If you have more angular features and prefer clothing and accessories that mimic this, then dramatic and edgy could be a style you gravitate towards.

Do you love how sharp you can look with the right accessories and outfit? Do you love the rebellious and mysterious effect clothes can play when you wear them? Do you live for the drama that high-contrast bold blacks, reds, and whites have against your skin?

Geometric designs, crisp fabrics and structured or tailored outfits excite your senses. Think *statement pieces!*

Hair is often worn shorter or cut in a blunt fashion with very strong, solid lines. Makeup is strong. Eye makeup may include a heavier eyeliner and often smokey eye and sharp contouring to highlight their angles.

Accessories include pointed-toed stilettoes, bags with structured edges leather, studs/rhinestones and animal prints.

When Glamour Meets Gratitude

Showing Up and Your Sense of Style

However you choose to show up today, being able to communicate your personal sense of style with the clothing you wear and the way you wear your hair and makeup will be a great way to express who you really are to others. I hope that having an understanding of the fundamentals of the design process when it comes to composing your artwork has given you a much stronger sense of clarity around how you choose to show up and why certain things will work on your body and why some things jar.

The more you play with the elements of tone and colour, line, texture, print, accents and mood, the better you will become at pulling them all together into a balanced, harmonious and cohesive style that reflects a more authentic expression of who you really are to the world.

Keep playing until you discover a composition you love.

Chapter 19

The final touches—Personal Creativity, Doing what you love, Self-Worth and Sharing yourself with others

If you've made it this far into the book you will certainly have a lot of newfound information swirling around in your head.

We've discussed the importance of gratitude for every part of your body. It is your lifelong vehicle and, in terms of fashion, it is your canvas. As such you must honour it and send love to each part of it through how you adorn it, take care of it and appreciate it.

We've also explored the value of being resourceful when it comes to your wardrobe, taking the time to value and embrace what you already have. You've learned how to make the most of it, including making sure that any new additions prove their worth in order to enter the exclusive domain of your wardrobe.

In the section on measuring up and fitting in, we acknowledged that the only measuring up that needs to occur is against yourself, not others. You were shown how to measure yourself for the best fit for your proportions. And you learned that attempting to fit in to other people's expectations of who you should be will only push you further away from a true sense of connection and belonging because, in essence, it pushes you away from you!

Finally, you were given a blueprint for how to show up in a way that reflects your true essence. Using the principles of art, design and composition you can now look at any outfit or garment and have an understanding of how it will impact your body (your canvas) and whether it will suit the style that you are wanting to express.

We only have a few more ingredients to add to this recipe before my job here is done. The rest will be up to you.

FINAL TOUCHES

Like adding a pinch of salt or pepper to a meal, developing these following qualities will imbue you with a flavour and essence that creates a true wow factor, that leaves an impact and makes you memorable. These final and essential ingredients are:

- Personal creativity

- Discovering and developing the things you truly love

- Increasing your feeling of self-worth

- Sharing your gifts with others.

PERSONAL CREATIVITY

Personal creativity is one quality that can never be taken away from you. Somebody may steal your idea, but they can never tap into the river that it flows from, which is you. It is your primary quality that will set you apart from others, because it's a form of self-expression that is uniquely your own.

So, how do you tap into and strengthen your never-ending flow of creativity? Below are three ways to get you started.

Stay curious

If you feel that you know everything, you stop growing. You can see this in personal styling when, for example, someone keeps the same hairstyle they had back in their 20s — and they're now in their 50s — because it worked for them back then. Be curious as to what works now. If it's been five years and you have the same hairstyle, perhaps a discussion with a decent hairdresser wouldn't go astray. Based on their suggestions you could then take a look at different celebrities with this style and play with how this look could work on you. Check whether the suggested haircut would suit your face shape (see Chapter 15). This also applies to your current wardrobe and in particular your accessories collection. How could an update in your accessories department refresh your wardrobe?

What are others doing?

This may seem to fly in the face of what I've been saying about not trying to fit in or gain others' approval. But this advice comes from a completely different place, as there's a big difference between inspiration and comparison. It's not about putting yourself down as you look at the other person, but about celebrating what they've done well. What you're doing is acknowledging the beauty and creative ways in others; the more you do this, the more these qualities will grow within you.

Next time you walk down the street, look around for what is beautiful in others. What are they doing that really works? They might have the perfect red lip colour to match their skin tone. Perhaps they're wearing a top that makes their eyes sparkle. The lines on their outfit might make them look taller, or distract from an area of their body that they would prefer to downplay. Perhaps they have managed to pull their style together with one or two key accessories that make the outfit pop. Work out how you could make elements that you admire on others work for you.

Create an inspiration board

There isn't a single artist in history who hasn't been inspired by something outside themselves. It may have been the way that colours come together in nature. It may have been the way that light hits certain objects and how that object reflects it back. It may have been textures, in fabrics or in the smoothness of a pebble. It may have been about the contrasts between sizes, colours or forms of objects. It may be the way that the eye is drawn in a specific direction based on how lines are placed.

When something grabs your attention, makes you stop and say 'I like that!', take a picture, or find an image that recalls it. Your attention could be drawn by fashion, architecture, nature, colour, print and pattern, trinkets, animals or plants. Start putting together an inspiration board based on what you like. This will give you a better idea of your personal sense of beauty and innate style. By focusing on the objects you are naturally drawn to, you will begin to see patterns. You can integrate these patterns not only into your wardrobe, but also your home and any other area of your life that you're able to adorn. This will make you feel happier, because you'll start feeling more integrated in all of the spaces you inhabit.

DO MORE OF WHAT YOU LOVE

Believe it or not, doing what you love is one of the most effective ways of building self-esteem and confidence. By focusing on what you love, you are able to ignore the constant marketing messages of 'not enough-ness' that pervade our modern society. This 'not enough-ness' may also come from your family or peers; there may be comparisons and expectations that are hurled at you on a regular basis.

A lot of people become caught up in worrying about what everyone else thinks about them. They do this to the extent that they don't even attempt to follow their heart's passions. They fill their schedules with everybody else's needs and agendas, and then complain they don't have time to learn that new skill or try that new thing they've always wanted to do. This is quite sad: by doing this they are telling themselves that they aren't worthy of happiness.

If you're used to running around for everybody else and it's really scary to block out time in order to meet your own needs, put it all in context. Give yourself just two hours, out of the 168 hours in a week, to learn or do something you love. You could start asking for more when you get braver, but for the moment venture into your new hobby, interest or passion by dedicating a minimum of two hours to it per week, *every* week. Doing this at the same time and same place each time will help turn the practise into a habit, and then a ritual.

Whether its knitting, tai chi or gardening, find your passion and keep coming back to it. You'll know when you love something because it's the thing that makes you feel that you want to explore it more deeply, more fully. Exploring your passion will help you to expand and grow. It's a natural process, like falling in love.

When you love something or somebody, it (or they) become completely fascinating, and you become very present with it or them. Interestingly, these attributes are considered by Olivia Cabanne-Fox, an expert in charisma, to be the main factors in making a person more charismatic. She explains that the most charismatic people display presence and a genuine warmth when they are with others, and that the best way to enhance your charisma is to become genuinely fascinated by others *

If you're already practising these skills, by spending your free hours doing things that you love, you'll actually find it a lot easier to be charismatic than your apathetic sisters. How so? You're developing your love muscle by throwing yourself into your passion projects. It's important to remember that whenever you make a change in one area of your life, it has an impact on other areas too.

Those who don't share your hobby or interest might tell you that something can't be done: how difficult it is to play the violin or sing, for example. However, you no longer feel the same way because you've taken the time and effort to understand your craft. Your curiosity and interest, and your desire to become better, hone your skills and understand your passion, whether it's a craft, instrument, garden, kitchen, body, voice, study or pet, far outweigh the obstacles.

What you gain in the process is insight, and a certain level of proficiency in the subject or skill that others don't have.

The objective here is to understand what it is that your heart calls out for and then pursue it. This will lead you to a fulfilled life. Following what everybody else tells you, you should love or do, instead, will not lead to the same outcome.

Knowing what you love will help to allow criticisms and external expectations to slide off you. If someone tells you that your beloved dog is ugly, you don't take in what they have to say. You can see the beauty in your dog: whatever anybody else says about it is irrelevant. If anything, it will make you bond more with your pet. The name-caller is the one with the issue, not you, and definitely not your dog!

You try on a skirt or dress that you love, and somebody tells you its ugly. 'To hell with them!' you think. 'They've clearly got no taste whatsoever.' You walk away from such pettiness, all the while reaffirming your love for your skirt.

Take a stand for everything you love in your life. When you're doing or following what you love, you'll suddenly find that you don't require external validation.

Another benefit of following your heart is that it helps bring out your inner beauty. By giving yourself the space to learn something new, you are telling the universe that you wish to develop, grow and create. Since mother nature is all about creation and growth, as you continue to develop yourself through the passion projects you choose, a beautiful personal unfolding occurs that is only given to those who follow their hearts.

Following your heart and doing what you love will make you a genuinely more loving individual. It will raise your energy as it brings you into the here and now. Take this new skill set into the community. Show the same level of attention, curiosity and fascination to others as you do towards your passion. Give people your full focus, pointing and positioning your entire body towards them, and you will be amazed at what follows.

People you never thought you could get along with suddenly really want to know you. People that previously didn't have that much to offer you suddenly start showing how amazing, loving and powerful they are. How did this happen? You gave them the space, time and attention to show you who they really are. And you need to learn to be this way with yourself too. Give yourself the attention, patience and permission to show up as you truly are. This is how you become authentically beautiful. When you show up fully present you will not only turn people's heads, you'll turn their hearts.

SELF-WORTH

Self-worth is extremely important, and it overlaps with doing what you love. Doing more of what you love helps you strengthen your self-worth muscle. It's not about becoming the best at something; the transformation comes from taking the time to please yourself, instead of everyone around you. This may sound selfish but in fact it is the opposite. Pleasing yourself first allows you to bring more of the real you to the table. The more you can truly love yourself, the more you will be able to love others.

You may think that self-sacrifice is loving, and at times it can be. However, having an unfulfilled life and an unhappy heart isn't showing genuine love to others. Do things because you love to do them, rather than for the validation or recognition. The more self-pleasing activities you do, the more you can block out external noise and live a life that is aligned with who you truly are, which is the ultimate form of service.

Recognise your value

We've covered how amazing your body is and how magnificently it works for you. It's now time to go a little deeper and list all of the natural abilities, character and physical qualities that you like about yourself or consider as strengths.

Think about all the knowledge and experience you've acquired over the years, and all the advice you offer others. You may not give it much thought because you offer it so naturally. You may even dismiss your knowledge and ability and say 'Anyone could do that.' Why isn't everybody doing it then?

Give these matters your full attention. Set aside time to express appreciation for your gifts and physical attributes, as well as the people that you love, the places you like to be, or even the things you like to tinker with.

Look in the mirror, starting at the top of your head. Do you like your hair? If so, how could you make more out of it? Could you try a new hairstyle? Perhaps apply a hair mask to nourish it? Learn how to braid it. Spend a couple of hours studying how to curl it and then try the uncomfortable bit: putting your learning into practise. Do it at least three times before giving in. Then come back the following week and try again.

Do you like your eyes? What could you learn about eyeshadow application in an allotted timeframe? Could you play with some makeup for a couple of hours, even if you get it completely wrong at first? Come back the following week and practise applying winged liner. Everything takes practise to master. Become the master of embellishment.

Continue going through each area of the body, looking solely for the things you like about yourself. Then dedicate an allotted amount of time each week to working out ways that you can improve the appearance of these areas through styling, hair and makeup.

This exercise can be extended to your natural skill sets. Take them to the next level, then consider how you can better share them with others.

Embrace your imperfections

Perhaps you did the exercise above. Maybe you enrolled in a makeup class. Maybe it was a painting, dancing or jewellery making class. And maybe you didn't excel.

If you're learning amongst others, it's easy to look around and think that everybody else is doing better than you. They seem to be understanding the instructions faster, or just seem to get the lesson better than you do. I can pretty much guarantee, however, that if you take a proper look at yourself there will be *at least* one way that you excel at what you're doing.

If you're painting, your draftsmanship might not be as great as the person sitting next to you in class, but your compositional arrangement, tonal work or colour combining might be better. If you're dancing, you might feel you have two left feet, but your posture, presence and gracefulness may outshine the person with all the fancy footwork.

The same principle applies to your wardrobe and makeup. Even if you feel like the biggest dag on the planet, there is always something you're getting right. You have an innate awareness that you haven't paid enough attention to because you were too busy comparing yourself to others.

Take a new look at yourself and recognise what you're doing well in the fashion and beauty department. You might be great at picking the right shade of lipstick or eyeshadow, or accessorising. You might be great at finding a garment that falls well on your figure. Maybe you don't have a logical explanation behind why, but intuitively you understand what works.

Wherever your interest lies, there's always some way in which you shine. So, the next time you look at 2–3 hours of labour and find yourself underwhelmed by the outcome, step back and ask yourself 'What is working here?' Examine yourself, section by section. You might need to take a photo or create a journal of your work, or even video it. Keep asking 'What is working?' and 'How can I repeat that in the next project, artwork, performance or recipe?' Then apply this skill set to your wardrobe and styling. What am I doing right? What works? What do I need to improve on? What do I need to learn?

You don't need to be perfect 24/7. As the meme says: 'It's not about being perfect, it's about being awesome'. Awesome is creating something amazing, something that 'perfect' can never be. Perfect is B-O-R-I-N-G! Unfortunately, too many people feel they need to be a perfect everything: have perfect skin, perfect hair, perfect outfits, perfect houses, perfect lawns, perfect manners, perfect responses, perfect bodies, perfect jobs. I could go on forever but you get my drift. Perfect appears to have become a societal construct, something to aim towards or aspire to. Aiming for perfect when you first start something is a recipe for disaster, because perfection is an external measurement against which you'll be judging your actions as you try to get better. Perfection comes from outside of you; its goal is to never let you achieve it and to stop you from discovering just how incredibly awesome you are.

Awesome, on the other hand, expresses the love of your craft as you improve. No judgement, just pure expression of loving, focused and creative energy.

You can strive for better but remember that you're already perfect, that you come from a state of completeness. Awesome is about loving what you do wholeheartedly, loving what you're passionate about. This also applies each day when you stand and look in the mirror. Don't aim for perfection when you dress yourself each morning; aim for awesome!

SHARING YOUR PASSIONS WITH OTHERS

When it comes to developing your creative talents, the final lesson is about sharing your skills or learning with others. This may be confronting because it's where you know you'll be judged. However, it is a necessary part of your general personal development.

When I first started painting, I took every single available class. I experimented with a large number of techniques and had a few successes as well as a handful of 'non-masterpieces'. I'd decided to go to college and hone my skills, and was in the second year of a three-year Diploma.

By this stage, I'd created a body of work and wanted to hang it on the walls of my business premises. At the time I owned a beauty salon. As this was the first time I was planning to hang my artwork publicly, I was a little apprehensive. I aired my concerns to Michael, my art teacher at the time, asking 'Am I ready? Or do I need more work? I'm a little scared; do you think it's good enough to hang?'

Michael's response will stay with me forever. He said, 'When it comes to displaying your work, what you have to do is the following. You take your work and you stand with it and you say, "Hi, I'm Jenny, and this is what I love to do". And that's it! People will then either give praise, criticism or indifference, and at the end of it all it doesn't really matter because you're still who you are, doing what you love to do, regardless.'

If you apply this philosophy to all of your new endeavours, including in your wardrobe and makeup, I promise that you'll start to see the truth of this. It's not about whether people will like or dislike what you do or how you present yourself; it's about doing what you love to do and then standing by it, come what may.

Keep doing what you love. Keep expressing who you truly are. Create space and time to do what you are passionate about, and soon enough you'll find that you become love — and that is a truly beautiful way to be.

Resources

Chapter 4

https://www.ilovejeans.com/apple-shape/
https://www.heddels.com/dictionary/yoke/

Chapter 5

Tomina Edmark - www.herroom.com

Chapter 6

https://www.neverdressdown.com/how-to-wear-a-backless-dress-without-a-bra/
https://www.bustle.com/articles/157485-11-ways-to-wear-a-backless-dress-with-big-boobs-because-your-breasts-deserve-the-best

Chapter 8

https://bustyresources.fandom.com/wiki/Bra_anatomy
https://www.abrathatfits.org/calculator.php
https://www.youtube.com/watch?v=8Jk55ep4XUQ

http://www.womenshealthmag.com/style/best-neckline-for-your-body/slide/14

https://www.gorgeautiful.com/knowing-the-right-necklines-for-your-face-and-body-shape-part-1/

https://www.joyofclothes.com/style-advice/clothing-guides/necklines/advice_and_ideas_for_the_most_popular_necklines.php

https://www.renttherunway.com/theshift/types-of-necklines

Chapter 9

https://insideoutstyleblog.com/2010/09/how-to-minimize-wide-or-square-shoulders.html

https://www.wiseshe.com/how-to-hide-broad-shoulders/

https://sewguide.com/kimono-sleeves-pattern/

Chapter 10

http://www.ebay.com/gds/How-to-Accessorise-an-Outfit-With-Bracelets-/10000000177320904/g.html

www.bollywoodshaadis.com

https://en.mimi.hu/jewelry/link_bracelet.html

https://www.rebelsmarket.com/blog/posts/the-ultimate-guide-on-how-to-accessorize-with-bracelets

https://www.thecharmworks.com/HistoryofCharms

https://www.heartmath.org/articles-of-the-heart/love-advanced-mode-intelligence/

Chapter 12

F Strack 1, L L Martin, S Stepper "Inhibiting and facilitating conditions of the human smile: a nonobtrusive test of the facial feedback hypothesis" Universität Mannheim, Federal Republic of Germany

Chapter 14

*R.N Clark https://clarkvision.com/ imagedetail/eye-resolution.html
*Rubin, Zick. "Lovers and Other Strangers: The Development of Intimacy in Encounters and Relationships: Experimental Studies of Self-Disclosure between Strangers at Bus Stops and in Airport Departure Lounges Can Provide Clues about the Development of Intimate Relationships." American Scientist, vol. 62, no. 2, 1974, pp. 182–190. JSTOR, www.jstor.org/stable/27844813. 2020
*Sandy Newbigging, creator of the Mind Calm technique
*Susan Krausse Whitbourne

Lovers and Other Strangers: The Development of Intimacy in Encounters and Relationships: Experimental studies of self-disclosure between strangers at bus stops and in airport departure lounges can provide clues about the development of intimate relationships on JSTOR

Zick Rubin, Lovers and Other Strangers: The Development of Intimacy in Encounters and Relationships: Experimental studies of self-disclosure between strangers at bus stops and in airport departure lounges can provide clues about the development of intimate relationships, American Scientist, Vol. 62, No. 2 (March-April 1974), pp. 182-190

Chapter 17

Justine Delacorte - http://recoveringshopaholic.com/the-dark-side-of-alterations/

Chapter 19

Olivia Fox Cabanne "The Charisma Myth: How to Engage, Influence and Motivate"